STEAMER FERRIES OF THE NORTHERN ISLES

ALISTAIR DEAYTON

AMBERLEY

First published 2015

Amberley Publishing
The Hill, Stroud
Gloucestershire, GL5 4EP

www.amberley-books.com

British Library Cataloguing in Publication Data.
A catalogue record for this book is available from the British Library.

ISBN: 978 1 8486 8921 3 (print)
ISBN: 978 1 4456 3704 4 (ebook)

Typeset in 10pt on 12pt Sabon.
Typesetting and Origination by Amberley Publishing.
Printed in the UK.

Contents

	Introduction	4
1	The North Company: Pre-1914	5
2	The North Company: 1914–1945	23
3	The North Company Post-War: 1945–1973	34
4	The Car Ferry Era	41
5	Northlink: 2002 to Present Day	55
6	Competitors and Chartered Vessels	58
7	Orkney Inter-Island Steamers and Ferries	81
8	Shetland Inter-Island Steamers and Ferries	109
	Acknowledgements	127

Introduction

The story of the steamers and ferries serving the Northern Isles of Orkney and Shetland, and of those operating within each island group, is long and complex.

The services from mainland Scotland to the islands were, from before the dawn of steam navigation right up until 2002, in the hands of the North of Scotland, Orkney & Shetland Shipping Company, known as the North Company, whose predecessors dated back to 1790 and which became part of the P&O Ferries group in 1975. The story is told of a succession of steamers, some very short-lived, some long-lived, and of motor vessels since 1939, and car ferries from 1975 onwards. The services were taken over in 2002 by Northlink; the story of their ferries is also told here. The waters around the islands and in the Pentland Firth are treacherous, and, especially in the era before the advent of radar, brief details of the loss of various steamers through shipwreck are told.

There have been only a handful of competitors over the years on these long routes, most of these short-lived. Over the years, the North Company has chartered a good number of vessels: in the Second World War, the naval traffic to Scapa Flow necessitated the use of a number of vessels outside the main fleet, allocated by the Ministry of War Transport. The story of all these vessels is told here in brief, as is the charter of livestock carriers after the demise of North Company's cargo vessels as well as those of the competing services across the Pentland Firth.

The islands of Orkney had their own steamer services, with many small operators serving individual islands, the North Isles being the exception to the rule, where the Orkney Steam Navigation Company operated from 1868 onwards. In the present era, Orkney Ferries connect all the islands to mainland Orkney. The story of all these vessels is told in word and picture.

Inter-island services in Shetland were operated for many years by the North Company's two steam and diesel *Earls of Zetland*. An overland route by bus and motor boat was established in the 1930s to Yell and Unst. Since 1974, the ferry fleet of Shetland Islands Council has served the islands. Services to the isolated islands of Foula and Fair Isle have not been forgotten in this survey of the steamers and ferries of the Northern Isles.

Chapter 1

The North Company: Pre-1914

Brilliant (1825) wrecked and on fire at Aberdeen's North Pier, 12 December 1839.

For many years (from 1875 to 1975), the North of Scotland, Orkney & Shetland Steam Navigation Company operated, almost without exception, the shipping services from Leith and Aberdeen to Orkney and Shetland. The so-called 'North Company' was formed in 1875, having its origins in the age of sail in 1790 as the Leith & Clyde Shipping Company, which had merged in 1820 with the Aberdeen, Dundee & Leith Shipping Company, thus forming the Aberdeen, Leith, Clyde & Tay Shipping Company; the word Tay being dropped from the title soon afterwards. In 1919, it became a limited company; in 1953, the word 'Shipping' replaced 'Steam Navigation' to reflect the increasing use of motor vessels. In 1961, the firm was taken over by Coast Lines Limited, but continued operating under its own name until 1975 when, Coast Lines having been absorbed into the P&O Group, it started operating under the P&O Ferries banner, and under P&O Scottish Ferries from 1989. In 2002, following the tendering process instigated for ferry services by the European Union, Northlink won the contract and replaced P&O on the services to the Northern Isles. Northlink was then under the ownership of the Caledonian MacBrayne group, but on the second renewal of its tender in 2012, ownership passed to the Serco Denholm group.

To get back to the beginnings of steam navigation to the Northern Isles, this began with *Velocity*, a paddle steamer built in 1821 by William Denny and Alexander McLachlan at Dumbarton, with an engine from the Greenhead Foundry, for the Aberdeen & Leith Steam Yacht Company. In 1825, competition arrived in the form of the Leith & Aberdeen Steam Yacht Company, operating a paddle steamer named *Brilliant* that was built by J. Lang & Co. in Dumbarton. In 1826, both steamers operating from Aberdeen to Newhaven (although *Brilliant* extended some of her sailings to Inverness), were taken over by the Aberdeen, Leith & Clyde Company, which had previously operated sailing smacks on the route. *Brilliant* operated each Tuesday from Newhaven to Aberdeen and Inverness from 1829 until her loss. Sailings were occasionally extended to Wick, this becoming a regular fortnightly run in summer 1833, when *Velocity* extended her trips to Kirkwall, giving Orkney her first taste of steam navigation. *Brilliant* was wrecked and destroyed by fire on 12 December 1839 when she hit Aberdeen's North Pier. Her captain had been washed overboard off Girdle Ness, and, on arrival at Aberdeen, she ran onto the pier. The lack of intake water for the boilers led them to overheating and setting the surrounding woodwork, and eventually the entire ship, on fire.

In the early days of steamer service, Newhaven was used as an alternative to Leith for a while.

Velocity was sold in 1844 to the Aberdeen & Newcastle Steam Navigation Company, and was also stranded on Aberdeen Pier, in her case on 25 October 1848.

A new steamer, *Sovereign*, built by John Wood at Port Glasgow, entered service in 1836 and made weekly departures in the summer months from Leith to Aberdeen, Wick, and Kirkwall, continuing to Lerwick on alternate weeks. In 1838, a government mail contract was awarded for a weekly mail service to Shetland between April and October and a service by sailing ship during the winter months. The service now left Leith on a Friday, a sailing which continued for 101 years until 1939, with the call at Wick omitted after 1891. *Sovereign* continued to operate for the company until being sold in 1865. She was laid up until 1872 when she was sold to Arklow owners and converted to a sailing ship. Her end came on 7 January 1905 when she was wrecked at Muros, Spain.

A new steamer, *Duke of Richmond*, also built by John Wood, entered service in summer 1838, replacing *Brilliant* on the summer Inverness service. She was on the Leith to Lerwick route in November 1838, but this only continued until the end of the year. She remained on the summer Inverness service until 1852 and was then on the Lerwick service until 1857. During the summers of 1858 and 1859, she was on the Leith–Wick service. On 8 October 1859, she ran ashore near the mouth of the River Don and was a total loss.

Bonnie Dundee had been built in 1837 by T. Adamson at Dundee for the Dundee & Leith Steam Packet Company and was purchased by the Aberdeen, Leith & Clyde Company in 1840. She was on the Aberdeen–Leith service with occasional sailings to Inverness and to Lerwick. She was sold in 1853 to the Maryport Steamship Company and was broken up in 1856.

The first *Queen* was built for the company by Simpson at Aberdeen in 1845. She ran from Leith to Inverness during the summer until 1847, was then on the Leith–Lerwick run from 1848 to 1852, and again served Inverness from 1853 to 1856. On 19 April 1857, she struck the Carr Rock en route from Aberdeen to Leith and was beached at Crail, where she broke up in a storm six days later.

Victory, which had been built in 1844 by Richard Dixon at South Shore, Gateshead, was purchased in 1847 and sold in 1860 to Liverpool owners.

Newhaven, which had been built in 1847 by John Jenkins Thompson at the Horseferry Dock at Rotherhithe for the Brighton & Continental Steam Packet Company, was purchased in 1849 and ran from Leith to Aberdeen in the summer months until she was sold in August 1851 to London owners.

In 1850, a weekly service was instituted from Leith to Wick; from 1852 it was extended to Scrabster and became known as the Caithness service, continuing until 1939. From 1870 until around 1900 it was extended occasionally to Stornoway. From July 1884, a fortnightly call at St Margaret's Hope was added to this service. A second weekly sailing to Wick was added from 1891. From 1898 the service was extended to Loch Eriboll.

The previous vessels had all been wooden-hulled paddle steamers, but the 1858 *Prince Consort* was the first iron-hulled steamer in the fleet. Built by J. & G. Thomson at Govan, she ran from Leith to Lerwick in the summer from 1858 until 1867 when, on the morning of 11 May, she ran aground in fog on Alten Rock, opposite the village of Burnbank near Cove. She broke into three pieces and sank within half an hour; fortunately there was no loss of life. Up until 1858 the steamer service had only run in the summer months, but from that date it became year round.

Another iron paddle steamer, *Hamburg*, was built by Robert Napier at Govan in 1849 and was sold three years later to Grimsby owners. She was re-purchased by the Aberdeen, Leith & Clyde Company in 1860 and ran from Leith to Wick year round for the next couple of years. She ran aground on Scotstoun Head near Peterhead en route from Kirkwall to Granton on 17 October 1862 and broke in two.

The Inverness service ceased in 1859 as a through rail route had been completed in the previous year between Aberdeen and Inverness.

The screw steamer *Queen* was built in 1861 by Smith & Rodger at Port Glasgow. She was initially on the Caithness service, was on the second summer service to Shetland from 1866 to 1871, and then served on a variety of services, most often on the West Side service. She was sold to Turkish owners in 1911, again in 1917 to Italian owners and was then seized while at Sebastopol during the Russian Revolution in 1917 and subsequently broken up.

The 20-year-old iron paddle steamer *Vanguard*, built by Robert Napier at Govan, was purchased in 1863 and was on the Wick service until 1867, apart from the summer of 1863 and a part of summer 1867 when she operated to Lerwick. She was broken up in 1868.

From summer 1866 to October 1879 Granton was used in place of Leith.

In 1866, what became known as the Secondary Indirect Boat started, providing a Tuesday sailing from Granton to Aberdeen, Kirkwall and Lerwick.

St Magnus, the company's final paddle steamer, was purchased in 1867. She had been built by C. Mitchell & Co. of Low Walker on the Tyne in 1864 with engines by Robert Stephenson & Co. as *Waverley* for the North British Railway Company's services from Silloth, on the Solway Firth. She was re-engined in 1875 with a two-cylinder compound engine by C. Howden & Co. She was the only fore and aft two-funnelled steamer in the company's history and served on the Leith–Aberdeen–Kirkwall–Lerwick route in the summer months until 1903. She was then sold in the following year to Gibraltar owners who renamed her *Magnus*. She was broken up at Rotterdam in 1913. Her name was perpetuated in the fleet until 1989.

The screw steamer *St Clair*, the first of five vessels of that name, was built in 1868 by Randolph, Elder & Co. of Govan and was placed on the Wick service, which she served in the summer until 1914, and again from 1920 until 1936 and in certain winters. On 27 August 1914, she was in a collision with the battleship HMS *Belleropheron* while on a special voyage from Scalloway to Invergordon with 1900 live lambs and no passengers. Her bow was damaged, her foremast went over the side, and the bowsprit was smashed, but there were no injuries and the lambs were unharmed. She sailed safely for Wick. The repairs took six weeks and necessitated the fitting of twenty hull plates and a new stem, figurehead and bowsprit. On 9 January 1918 she was attacked by a surfaced German submarine and fired back. One of her gun crew was killed by a fragment of shell and the ship's cook was injured, later dying of his injuries. Captain William Leask, who had survived the sinking of *St Margaret* seven months previously, was in command. In 1936 she was renamed *St Colm* and sold for breaking up in Germany in 1937, after almost seventy years with the company.

St Nicholas was built in 1871 by J. G. Lawrie & Co. of Whiteinch, with engines by James Howden & Co. and served mainly on the Wick service and the West Side service until she ran aground at the entrance to Wick Harbour on 17 June 1914 and was lost.

Black's *Guide to Scotland* in 1877 advertised three regular services:

Mondays: Granton–Aberdeen–Wick–Thurso (i.e. Scrabster)
Tuesdays: Granton–Aberdeen–Kirkwall–Lerwick
Fridays: Granton–Aberdeen–Wick–Kirkwall–Lerwick

In 1881, a third weekly sailing to Shetland was started in the summer months, this time to the west coast, calling at Scalloway and the smaller communities of Spiggie, Walls, Brae, Voe, Aith and Hillswick, leaving Leith on a Monday and calling at Aberdeen and Stromness en route. This, known as the West Side service, was maintained until 1939. Unadvertised calls were made at Reawick and at Roeness Voe. Scalloway and Walls were the only ports with piers, and the remainder of the calls were made fortnightly or even monthly. The steamer also called at St Margaret's Hope on the way south for much of the period of operation.

After the St Magnus Hotel had been built at Hillswick in 1902, or in fact reassembled there after being prefabricated in Norway and being on display at the Great Exhibition at Glasgow in 1896, this was sold as a tourist route with a week-long stay in the hotel. The hotel continued to be owned by the company until sold in 1972. Around the same time the Standing Stones Hotel was built for the company at Stenness in Orkney; the hotel was owned by the company until the late 1950s.

In 1883, the North Company took over the Scrabster to Stromness service across the Pentland Firth from the Highland Railway. The steamer *St Olaf*, which had been built in the previous year by Murdoch & Murray of Port Glasgow, with engines by Dunsmuir & Jackson of Govan, operated the service but was sold in 1890 to Quebec owners, where she was lengthened by 20 feet and sold again in 1893. She ran aground and was lost near the mouth of Seven Islands Bay, Labrador on 21 November 1900.

The first *St Rognvald* was built in 1883 by Hall Russell of Aberdeen, who would become the company's first choice of builders for the next fifty-six years, and operated on the weekend sailing to Lerwick. From 1886 she was on summer cruises to the Norwegian Fjords for about ten years. These were the first ever cruises by any shipping line from the UK, and the precursor of what is today a vast industry. She had a buff funnel during her years on cruising duty. On 24 April 1900, she was wrecked at Burgh Head, Stronsay.

The success of these cruises was such that a dedicated cruise steamer, *St Sunniva*, was built in 1887 by Hall Russell. Her accommodation was purely for passengers and she had triple expansion machinery. She had a clipper bow, figurehead and a buff funnel, whereas at that time the remainder of the fleet had black funnels. In 1908, she went onto the regular Lerwick service, cargo and mail accommodation was added and her funnel was painted black until after the First World War, when it reverted to buff. She continued after the First World War on the Lerwick service, twice-weekly from Aberdeen, one of these starting from Leith, until she ran aground at Mousa in fog on her way north from Aberdeen on the morning of 10 April 1930. After about a fortnight ashore she broke up.

In 1890, the North Company took over the Shetland Islands Steam Navigation Company, which operated from Lerwick to the North Isles of Shetland, and their steamer *Earl of Zetland*. She had been built in 1877 by John Fullerton & Co. at Paisley and had a very long career on the service. She also served as a relief steamer on the Pentland Firth service and made occasional trips prior to 1914 from Lerwick to Aberdeen and Leith, mainly with livestock. On 26 July 1912, she ran aground on the islet of Lunna Holm, at the mouth of Yell Sound, in fog. She put the women and children ashore there and managed to get the ship free at high tide, then she made for Burravoe in South Yell where she was beached just before sinking. About a dozen male passengers had remained on board and were served a meal, while the women on Lunna Holm had no meal and had to wait a few hours before the Burravoe flit-boat arrived to rescue them. *St Sunniva* arrived during the following night and took the passengers on to their destinations. The *Earl* was salvaged and returned to service. On 28 August 1924 she ran aground on the rock known as Robbie Ramsay's Baa outside Lerwick. The passengers were rescued by a fishing boat and the *Earl* remained stuck firm until pulled off by a salvage vessel a couple of days later. In 1939, anticipating the arrival of her successor with the same name, she was renamed *Earl of Zetland II*, but remained on the North Isles run throughout the war years and was sold in December 1946 to a Panama-flag owner, a cover for the Jewish organisation Aliyah Bet, with the aim of carrying illegal immigrants to what was then Palestine, now Israel. She sailed for Marseilles under the cover name *Anal* and was named *Yehuda Hahlevy*. She was the first steamer to bring immigrants from North Africa and left Algiers on 11 May 1947 with 399 passengers. She ran out of fuel on 18 May, and on 31 May she was surrounded by five British destroyers and boarded by soldiers. Her crew had sabotaged the engines, and she was towed to Haifa where she lay until scrapped in 1950.

In 1891 a twice-weekly direct Aberdeen–Lerwick service was started, a service which forms the mainstay of the route to this day.

In 1892 a new steamer, *St Ola*, was built by Hall Russell to replace *St Olaf* on the Scrabster–Stromness service. Unlike her predecessor, she had a very long life servicing the route until being broken up in 1951. Up to 1939 she also called at Scapa Pier, but improved roads following the war meant that a bus connection from Kirkwall to Stromness sufficed. During the Second World War she rescued five British officers, including a vice admiral, from an aircraft which had come down in the sea.

Also built by Hall Russell in 1892 was *St Giles*, which served on the direct Aberdeen to Lerwick service until she ran ashore near Rattray Point lighthouse on 28 September 1902 and broke her back.

The first *St Ninian* was built in 1895 by Ramage & Ferguson of Leith and was initially placed on the weekend service from Leith and Aberdeen to Kirkwall and Lerwick year round, but was moved to what was known as the Secondary Indirect Service in the summer months from 1897 right up to 1936, apart from 1914-1918 when she was under Admiralty control on the Pentland Firth crossing. From 1937 to 1939 she was on the Caithness service, including a call at St Margaret's Hope. She was used again in the Second World War as a transport for naval personnel between Scrabster and Longhope, continuing until December 1946, following which she was laid up at Aberdeen until broken up in 1948. During her second spell of war service, she crossed the Pentland Firth about 3,000 times, steaming over 100,000 miles and carrying some 900,000 service and other passengers.

From 1900 to 1905, the weekend sailing was extended to Baltasound.

A second *St Rognvald* was built in 1901 by Hall Russell to replace her wrecked predecessor of the same name. She was on the summer weekend run until 1924, apart from the war years, and again from 1946 to 1949. From 1937 to 1939 she was on the West Side service in the summer and, in the summer of 1950, ran from Leith and Aberdeen to Stromness. During the Second World War, she ran from Aberdeen to Orkney. She was scrapped in 1951.

A second *St Giles* was built in 1903 by Hall Russell for the direct service from Aberdeen to Lerwick, which she maintained until sold to the Government of Zanzibar in 1911. She was renamed *Psyche* and later *Khalifa*, and was used as the sultan's yacht until broken up in 1928.

The second *St Magnus* was built in 1912 by Ramage & Ferguson for the secondary indirect service. She was torpedoed and sunk by a German U-boat off Peterhead on 12 February 1918. She sank in about five minutes with the loss of five lives.

St Margaret, a larger sister of *St Magnus*, was built in 1913, also by Ramage & Ferguson. She was chartered to G. & J. Burns during the First World War to run from the UK to Iceland and was torpedoed and sunk by a U-boat thirty miles south-east of the Faeroes on 11 September 1917. Five crew members were drowned, and one lifeboat got away with four crew members. The other was capsized by suction as the ship went down and the remaining crew members, including Captain William Leask, were trapped underneath. The men in the first lifeboat broke through the hull of the capsized one and rescued the captain and the remainder of the trapped men, apart from a fireman who had died while awaiting being freed from the capsized boat. The crew then attempted to row the thirty miles into the wind to the Faeroes, but when Captain Leask regained conciousness, eight or nine hours later, decided to sail and row the 150 miles to the Shetlands instead, a sail having been improvised from part of the lifeboat's canvas cover and a mast from an oar. They eventually reached Hillswick after three days and nights in the open boat. Captain Leask was awarded the Distinguished Service Cross and Lloyds War Medal for this.

In 1913 the company's first cargo steamer, *St Fergus*, was built by Hawthorns & Co. of Leith. She has sold on the stocks to Argentinian owners, and was bought back from them in 1916. She had no passenger accommodation, and served the company until she sank after a collision off Rattray Head on 31 December 1940, with the loss of her master.

The paddle steamer *Queen* (1845).

The shipwreck of *Prince Consort* on 11 May 1867. Note the number of people on the beach.

The shipwreck of a paddle steamer on the beach at, or near, Aberdeen, probably *Prince Consort* (1858) on 11 May 1967.

The first *St Magnus*, formerly the North British Railway's Silloth-based *Waverley* of 1864, which served the North Company from 1867 to 1901, seen here alongside at Lerwick.

A painting of the paddle steamer *St Magnus*.

The dining saloon of the first *St Magnus*.

The first *St Clair* (1868) entering Wick harbour, with Langlands and Hain Line steamers in the background.

St Clair (1868) at Leith.

A postcard view of *St Nicholas* (1871).

North of Scotland,
Orkney, & Shetland
Steam Navigation
Company.

St. Magnus Hotel, Hillswick, Shetland.

This is the Hotel we stay at–as it is
the only one too. it is all of wood
both inside and out–but–Very
nice and Comfortable a little
too fashionable for Yours truly
Break fast–9 Luncheon 1–30.
Afternoon tea 4 Dinner 7–0

Opened 1900, under the Company's management, affords excellent accommodation for visitors at moderate rates. There is good and extensive loch and sea fishing in the neighbourhood. The coast scenery is grand. Tudor in his "Orkney and Shetland," published in 1883, page 533, says:—"When, as must come sooner or later, proper accommodation is provided throughout the length and breadth of Shetland for travellers in search of the beautiful, who will flock northwards, there will be no spot in all Hjaltland which in its manifold attractions will be so popular as 'Grey Hillswick.'" Apply to the Manageress of the Hotel, Hillswick.

A postcard view with vignettes of the company-owned St Magnus Hotel, Hillswick, and *St Nicholas* of 1871.

The 1877 *Earl of Zetland*, which served the North Isles of Shetland from her building right up to 1946.

The short-lived Pentland Firth steamer *St Olaf*, which only operated from 1883 to 1890.

The first *St Rognvald* of 1883, Britain's first cruise ship.

The first *St Sunniva* (1887) at Odda, in the upper reaches of the Hardangerfjord.

St Rognvald (1883) at Bergen on a cruise.

The first *St Ola* of 1892, berthed at Stromness.

SCAPA PIER, ORKNEY.   KENT'S SERIES

St Ola (1892), departing Scapa Pier.

The first *St Giles* of 1892 at Lerwick.

St Ninian of 1895 at Leith on 24 June 1934.

The second *St Rognvald* of 1903 in a watercolour by Alexander Harwood.

St Rognvald at Leith on 1 September 1934.

The second *St Giles* of 1903.

The first *St Margaret* of 1913, which only saw two summers' service and was sunk in the North Atlantic on 12 September 1917.

21. *St Fergus*

The cargo steamer *St Fergus* of 1913.

Chapter 2

The North Company: 1914–1945

G. & J. Burns' cargo steamer *Ape* of 1898, which became the North Company's first *Fetlar* in 1918, but only lasted for a few months before being wrecked in April 1919.

The cargo steamer *Temaire*, built in 1890 as *Burnock* for Ayr owners by S. McKnight of Ayr, with engines by W. Kemp of Glasgow, was purchased in 1916, but was sold at the end of the following year and survived under various owners until scrapped in 1931.

A second cargo steamer, *Cape Wrath*, was purchased in 1916. She had been built in 1900, also by McKnight of Ayr, with engines by Ross & Duncan, and served the company until 1927. She was stranded in the River Severn in 1932 and later broken up.

Express (see Chapter 6) was purchased in 1917 and was lost in a collision off the French coast on 4 April of that year. She had been built in 1865 by Readhead, Softley & Co. of South Shields for George Robertson of Kirkwall, and had operated from Kirkwall to Leith and Aberdeen since 1898, with an occasional charter for the Pentland Firth service.

The cargo steamer *Ape*, which had been built by Barclay Curle at Whiteinch for G. & J. Burns' Greenock–Belfast service in 1898 and sold by them in 1912, was purchased by the North Company in 1918 and renamed *Fetlar*. She sank on 13 April 1919 after striking a rock near St Malo. She was replaced by David MacBrayne's *Cavalier* of 1883, built by Aitken & Mansel at Whiteinch with engines by Muir & Caldwell, which was purchased in 1919 and also renamed *Fetlar*. She relieved on the North Isles service and was sold in 1920 and broken up in 1927.

After the First World War the funnels of the main passenger steamers were painted in yellow rather than black and the funnels of all ships built after 1937 were yellow.

Also purchased from MacBrayne in 1919 was *Chieftain*, a luxurious passenger ship which had been built in 1907 by Ailsa at Troon with machinery by the Clyde Shipbuilding and Engineering Company of Port Glasgow, for the Glasgow–Stornoway route. She was renamed *St Margaret* and placed on the West Side service serving the company's St Magnus Hotel at Hillswick. She was sold in 1925 to the Canadian National Steamship Company and renamed *Prince Charles*, and sold again in 1940 to the Union Steamship Company of British Columbia by whom she was named *Camosun*. She was again sold in 1945 to Tel Aviv owners who renamed her *Cairo* for the illegal immigrant trade to Palestine. In 1947 she was chartered to a Lebanese company and made one trip from Marseilles to Beira and was broken up at La Spezia in 1952.

St Magnus of 1924, built by Hall Russell, was the largest steamer built for the company so far. She operated the weekend summer sailing until 1939, apart from in 1930 when she was placed on the direct Aberdeen to Lerwick service following the loss of *St Sunniva*. Her first class accommodation was aft and she had a moveable bulkhead on the tween deck to enable part to be used for cattle and the remainder for passengers, the proportions varying depending on the amount of cattle on a particular sailing. She was requisitioned by the Admiralty in September 1939 and spent the war as a guard ship moored in Kirkwall Bay with occasional trooping voyages, including to Norway in April 1940, to Lerwick in May 1940 and from Lyness to Rosyth and also from Kirkwall to Aberdeen in June 1940. Post-war, she was initially on the main indirect service and was back on the weekend sailing from 1950, although this now only went as far as Kirkwall, apart from in the peak summer season. She was scrapped in 1960.

The company's first *St Clement*, also built by Hall Russell, was an engines-aft cargo steamer built in 1928. She operated the winter service to Wick and also relieved *Earl of Zetland* each autumn for overhaul. She was on various cargo routes for the remainder of the year and had accommodation for twelve passengers. She was sunk in an air attack 20 miles south-east of Peterhead on 5 April 1941.

Burns Laird's *Lairdsbank*, formerly Laird Line's *Olive*, built in 1893 by D. & W. Henderson at Glasgow, was purchased as a stopgap in 1930 to replace the sunken *St Sunniva* and was renamed *St Catherine*. She was on the West Side run in 1930, but her sleeping accommodation was inadequate for peak season traffic on any of the company's routes. She was then laid up in the summer months and was on the direct Aberdeen–Lerwick service in winter until being sold for breaking up in May 1937.

A second *St Sunniva* was launched on 2 April 1931 by Hall Russell, almost exactly a year after the loss of her predecessor. She was a magnificent clipper-bowed steamer with a white hull. She operated in the summer months on the direct Aberdeen–Lerwick service from 1931 until 1939. She served in the war years, initially as a guard ship and accommodation ship in Scapa Flow. In September 1942, she was converted to a convoy rescue ship and left Greenock on her first assignment on 3 January 1943 escorting a convoy to New York. She was lost on 22 January 1943, with all sixty-four crew and medical staff, two days out of Halifax, Nova Scotia. It is believed that her masts and rigging became iced up and she turned turtle and sank. Another ship on the same convoy had arrived at Halifax on the previous day with ice up to 10 feet thick in some parts.

The final steamer to be built for the company was the second *St Clair* in 1937, again by Hall Russell. She was slightly larger than *St Magnus* and ran to the west side of Shetland in summer and on the weekend service in winter. She continued to serve Shetland initially in the Second World War, but was requisitioned on 23 October 1940 and renamed HMS *Baldur*, being used as an accommodation and base ship moored in Reykjavik harbour. In October 1943, she was replaced in this duty by the Dover–Ostend steamer *Princesse Marie Jose*. She regained the name *St Clair* and was converted to a convoy rescue ship back at Aberdeen. She served as such from 1 July 1944 until the end of the war, working with fourteen convoys. When normal services resumed she went onto the Aberdeen–Lerwick direct service, which she maintained until 1960. She was then renamed *St Magnus* and was on the weekend service from Leith and Aberdeen to Kirkwall in summer and part of the winter. She was renamed *St Magnus II* in late 1966, then withdrawn on 1 April 1967 and immediately sold for scrapping.

The company's first motor vessel, the second *Earl of Zetland*, was built in 1939 by Hall Russell. Although built for the North Isles service, her early years were spent on the Pentland Firth crossing due to vastly increased traffic there serving the naval establishments on Scapa Flow. She came under military control, being used as a troop carrier and occasionally serving Lyness, Longhope, Flotta, St Margaret's Hope and Scapa as well as Stromness. In December 1945, she went onto the North Isles service with occasional sailings from Lerwick to Aberdeen in the first few months. She served the North Isles until the advent of the car ferries in 1973. In post-war years this comprised a Monday and Friday trip from Lerwick to Baltasound on Unst, returning on the following day; on Tuesdays via Skerries; a Wednesday return sailing from Lerwick to Uyeasound on Unst; a Thursday evening excursion in summer from Lerwick round Bressay and Noss, and occasional Sunday excursions to Fair Isle or Foula. The calls were gradually reduced as the car ferry routes came into operation between May 1973 and February 1975, when she was withdrawn from service.

She was sold to Middlesbrough Ocean Surveys for oil-related work and renamed *Celtic Surveyor*, only serving briefly in an operational role as such. She was laid up at Great Yarmouth for a few years and was sold to a local group for conversion to an entertainment centre, with bars and a dance floor, in 1983, where she was statically moored at the South Quay in Great Yarmouth. Her owners went into receivership within a couple of years and, in late spring 1986, she was moved to the West India Dock, London, where she opened as 'London's Underwater Museum'. This was not a success and in 1988 she was leased to City Fine Wines and opened as a wine bar in London's Docklands, becoming a bar/bistro/canteen for the staff of the *Daily Telegraph* at their new offices in the Isle of Dogs. In 1990 she was moved to Eastbourne's Sovereign Harbour marina, where in 1994 she regained her original name; on 1 February 1997, she was moved again to the Royal Quays Marina, North Shields, near the DFDS ferry terminal, where she remains to this day as a pub/restaurant. Her screw was removed when in London, moved to Eastbourne, and is now in the Shetland Museum.

1939 saw the purchase of the passenger-cargo steamer *Highlander* from the Aberdeen, Newcastle & Hull Shipping Company, a subsidiary of the Dundee, Perth & London Shipping Company Ltd. She had been built in 1916 by the Caledon Shipbuilding Company at Dundee. On 1 August 1940, she brought down two enemy planes whilst on passage from Aberdeen to Leith, arriving at Leith with the wreckage of one of them on her poop. She was renamed *St Catherine* and survived two more aerial attacks, but was sunk on 14 November 1940 by a torpedo launched from an aircraft off Aberdeen, with the loss of her captain, thirteen members of crew and one passenger, with three passengers and fourteen crew members being rescued.

Rora Head was another 1939 purchase. An engines-aft cargo steamer, she had been built by Day, Summers & Co. at Southampton in 1921 for the General Steam Navigation Company as *Blackcock* and sold in 1937 to Henry & McGregor of Leith and renamed. She operated on the Wick service after the war and, when that service ceased, she was sold out of the fleet in 1956 to Italian owners.

Another engines-aft cargo steamer, *Amelia*, was purchased in 1940. She had been built in 1894 by S. McKnight at Ayr, with engines by Muir & Houston. She had been owned by Cooper & Company of Kirkwall since 1920, operating a Kirkwall–Aberdeen and Leith cargo service, which she continued to operate until 1955 when she was found to be taking in water on a voyage from Leith to Kirkwall. She had to put into Aberdeen to avoid sinking and she was broken up in the following year.

Dunleary, another 1940 purchase for the cargo services, had been built in 1905 by A. & J. Inglis as a steam collier for Dublin owners. She was sold in 1946 to Greek owners, and was sunk off the coast of Cyrenaica on 17 September 1962 on a voyage from Greece to Benghazi.

The second *St Margaret*, formerly MacBrayne's *Chieftain* of 1907, purchased in 1919 and sold to Canadian owners in 1925. This photograph shows her partially repainted in North Company colours in 1919.

The third *St Magnus* of 1924, which was in the fleet until 1960.

The cargo steamer *St Clement* of 1928, which was sunk by an enemy air attack on 5 April 1941.

St Clement at Leith on 1 September 1934, painted with a grey hull at this stage.

The second *St Sunniva* of 1931 in a poster timetable image.

St Sunniva (1931), arguably one of the most beautiful British Coastal steamers of her era, in a company advertisement.

St Sunniva (1931) in a Real Photographs image.

The 1937 *St Clair* at Lerwick, Victoria Pier.

St Clair (1937) entering Aberdeen Harbour in a storm on 20 November 1950. This dramatic view shows the classic steamer being handled expertly by her helmsman in extreme weather conditions.

St Magnus, formerly *St Clair* (1937), at Leith around 1965.

Earl of Zetland (1939) at Mid Yell in 1968.

Earl of Zetland in her present location, adjacent to the North Sea ferry terminal at North Shields.

S.S. HIGHLANDER.

This luxurious Passenger Steamer sails Aberdeen to Newcastle & Hull every Saturday returning from Hull every Wednesday and from Newcastle every Thursday. ⁓ Aberdeen Newcastle & Hull Steam Co. Ld. Aberdeen. ⁓

An official Aberdeen, Newcastle & Hull Steam Co. postcard of *Highlander* of 1916, purchased by the North Company in 1939 and lost on 14 November 1940 in an air-launched torpedo attack.

The steam collier *Dunleary* (1906), owned by the North Company from 1940 until 1947.

Chapter 3

The North Company Post-War: 1945–1973

The cargo motor vessel *St Clement* (1946).

The first vessel to be built for the company after the Second World War was the cargo motor vessel *St Clement*, built in 1946 by Hall Russell. She also relieved on the Pentland Firth and North Isles services. She could carry twelve passengers and had berths for these in two-berth cabins in an accommodation block amidships. She had livestock ramps so that the animals could be unloaded directly from the upper (shelter) deck and another ramp from there to the main deck. Her usual pattern of sailings was livestock sailings from September to November, the secondary indirect service from Leith to Kirkwall from November to May, relief on the North Isles service in March and April and she was used as a back-up vessel in the remainder of the year. After the introduction of *St Rognvald* in 1955, she took over some of the former Cooper's sailings from Kirkwall and Stromness to Aberdeen. In the summer months from the mid-sixties until the advent of the car ferry *St Ola* in 1975, she served as a second vessel on the Scrabster to Stromness service, carrying mainly cars. Her final run was on 30 November

1976, returning to Aberdeen on 5 December. A week later she was sold to Greek owners, surviving there until broken up in 1984.

In 1950, the first twin screw vessel in the fleet, *St Ninian*, a passenger motor vessel, was built by Caledon at Dundee. She was placed on the indirect run, departing Leith on a Monday for Aberdeen, Kirkwall and Lerwick. She remained on that service until sold to Canadian owners in March 1971. She was not renamed and offered cruises from North Sydney, Nova Scotia to St Pierre and Miquelon in the summers of 1971 and 1972, and was then laid up for four years until sold for cruising in the Galapagos Islands in 1976. She was renamed *Bucanero* and later *Buccaneer* and, after a long spell laid up, was broken up in 1991.

1951 saw a new diesel *St Ola* for the Scrabster–Stromness crossing, built by Alexander Hall & Company at Aberdeen. She was like a slightly larger version of *Earl of Zetland* and served the route until replaced by the car ferry of the same name in January 1975, having been renamed *St Ola II* in autumn 1974. She was sold at the end of January 1975 for use as a seismic survey ship and renamed *Aqua Star*, working in the Mediterranean and off the east cost of Canada until being scrapped at Vigo in 1987.

A further cargo vessel, the third *St Rognvald*, was built in 1955 by Alexander Hall & Company at Aberdeen. It was originally proposed that she carry fifty passengers, but she was built with berths for only twelve passengers. Her accommodation was aft, compared to amidships for *St Clement*. She normally operated a spring/summer cargo service to Kirkwall, St Margaret's Hope and Stromness, and after it in winter on the secondary indirect service from Leith to Kirkwall and Stromness and, for part of the winter, the weekend service to Kirkwall. She also offered autumn livestock runs, with occasional calls at Baltaroud and Fetlar. Calls at St Margaret's Hope ceased in 1966 and at Stromness in 1971, by which time *St Rognvald* was on a Monday sailing from Aberdeen to Kirkwall and Lerwick, returning direct to Aberdeen. In 1972 a call at Kirkwall southbound was added to this sailing. On 4 May 1973, she ran aground on Thieves Holm in Kirkwall Bay and was not relocated until the 18th, returning to service after repairs on 25 June. She was sold in 1978 to Gibraltarian owners who renamed her *Winston* and converted her to carry containers by removing the cattle decks and adding securing points for the containers. She was then used on a service from Shoreham to Gibraltar, and was sold again in 1986 to Gambian owners. She was scrapped in 2000 after three further changes of name.

The final passenger vessel to be built for the company before the roro era was *St Clair*, which was built in 1960 by Ailsa at Troon. She was larger than *St Ninian*, but reverted to a single screw arrangement and was used on the direct Aberdeen to Lerwick service. In February of 1970 and 1971, she relieved the Belfast Steamship Company's *Ulster Queen* and *Ulster Prince* for a couple of weeks for overhaul as both companies were part of the Coast Lines Group, which had taken over the North Company in 1961. She was renamed *St. Clair II* in February 1977 and was sold to Kuwaiti owners in June 1977, her final sailing for the company having been southbound from Lerwick on 9 June. She was converted to the livestock carrier *Al Khairat* and was scrapped at Gadani Beach in Pakistan in 1987.

In 1966, the Dutch-built cargo vessel *City of Dublin* was purchased from Palgrave Murphy of Dublin and renamed *St Magnus*, becoming the fifth vessel of that name in the company's fleet. She replaced the last surviving steamer in the fleet,

St Magnus, ex *St Clair*, of 1937 when she entered service in April 1967. She made the final sailing to Leith on 9 March 1971. All sailings, apart from the Pentland Firth crossing, started from Aberdeen and from then on operated on a Thursday from Aberdeen to Kirkwall. She was sold in May 1977 to Cyprus owners, and sank after a collision at the entrance to the Black Sea on 12 January 1979.

The motor vessel *St Ninian* (1950), arriving at Leith.

St Ninian departing Leith *c.* 1965.

THE M.V. ST. OLA, AT SCRABSTER HARBOUR   *Copyright J. Adams*

The Pentland Firth motor vessel *St Ola* of 1951 at Scrabster.

St Ola as *Aqua Star*, laid up at Leith 1986.

Cargo motor vessel *St Rognvald* of 1955 off Aberdeen in 1964.

St Rognvald berthed at Aberdeen *c.* 1965.

St Clair at Aberdeen.

St Clair at Liverpool, 19 January 1971.

City of Dublin, soon to become *St Magnus*, at Aberdeen in 1966.

The cargo vessel *St Magnus* during her short spell with the company from 1966 to 1971.

Chapter 4

The Car Ferry Era

St Ola at Scrabster, with a blue funnel and black hull after 1976.

P&O Ferries 1975–2002

In 1974 a new *St Ola*, the third of the name, was built by Hall Russell at Aberdeen. She was a drive-through car ferry, the first to serve the Northern Isles. She was completed in October 1974, but lay at Stromness until the roll-on roll-off ramp was completed at Scrabster, and did not enter service until 29 January 1975. On 27 October 1982, she suffered an engine room fire on her return from overhaul on the Clyde, 4 miles south-west of Pladda, and had to be towed back to the Tail of the Bank. She did not return to service after repairs until 8 February of the following year. In early 1990, she was rebuilt with ugly side sponsons and a water tank above the wheelhouse to increase her stability and comply with the post-Zeebrugge rules. She served the route faithfully until 1992, when she was briefly named *St Ola II* on 23 March before being withdrawn and laid up at Leith a couple of days later. She was renamed *Cecilia* for a charter to Svenska Rederi Ab Kattegat of Helsingborg for a service from Helsingborg to Hundested in Denmark from 15 October 1992 until January 1993, then returning to Leith for lay-up. She was sold in April 1993 to Panama-flag owners and operated across the Adriatic from Otranto to Igoumenitsa in 1993 and the early part of 1994, under the name *Odigitria*, for Ventouris Sea Lines; she was sold to the Chinese Government in 1995, after which the trail runs cold.

In February 1971, Coast Lines had been taken over by the P&O Group, and in March 1975, *Lion*, from the Ardrossan to Belfast service of Burns Laird Lines, was considered for transfer to the North Company, and tenders were put out for work to convert her for the Aberdeen to Lerwick service. At the beginning of October 1975, the company was renamed P&O Ferries (Orkney and Shetland services) and the funnel of *St Ola* was repainted in pale blue.

The freight roro vessel *Helga I* was purchased in 1975 and renamed *ROF Beaver*, *ROF* signifying Roll On-Off. She had been built in 1971 by D. W. Kremer at Elmshorn in Germany as *Bibiana* for a German operator. Her stern ramp enabled her to discharge onto a quayside. She inaugurated the new Holmsgarth terminal at Lerwick in June 1976. Her sailings were normally in connection with the newly-fledged oil exploration industry and she mainly ran to Sullom Voe and Lerwick until 24 March 1983. On 11 April 1985 she sailed, unusually, from Leith, via Granton and Ardersier, to Lerwick. She was sold in 1987 to Torbay Seaways, for whom she ran as *L. Taurus* from Torquay to the Channel Islands. She was sold again in 1990, undergoing several changes of name and ownership in the ensuing years and being broken up at Aliaga in Turkey in 2012.

The car ferry *SF Panther* of P&O Southern Ferries was transferred for the Lerwick service, where she commenced operation on 4 April 1977 under the name *St Clair*. She had been built in 1965 at the Flender-Werke in Lübeck, Germany for Travemünde-Trelleborg Line as *Peter Pan* for the route between these ports, being sold to Southern Ferries and renamed *SF Panther* in 1973 for the Southampton to San Sebastian service, which closed in November 1975. In December 1975 she had been chartered to Da-No Line for the service from Oslo to Aarhus as *Terje Vigen*. On 14 January 1981, she was hit by a huge wave about 34 miles north of Rattray Head, which blew in the bridge windows and disabled the steering gear and radar. She managed to get under way again using manual steering after about fifteen minutes, and was able to return to Aberdeen safely. In 1982 she started what was to become an annual charity cruise in mid-May from Lerwick round Bressay and Noss. On 19 May 1983, she made a special trip from Aberdeen to Gothenburg to convey passengers for the European Cup's Winners' final, where Aberdeen beat Real Madrid, returning to Aberdeen in triumph on 23 May. On 30 September 1983, her Lerwick weekend mini-cruise was extended to Bergen, with two nights ashore there. 350 passengers were carried, all but forty joining at Lerwick. On 1 May 1987, she operated a two-night cruise from Aberdeen to Scheveningen in the Netherlands, and on 15 May 1987 she made a mini-cruise to Bergen via the Hardangerfjord, returning on 19 May. She had a special charter on 7 October 1990 for the centenary of the Forth Bridge, being used as a Royal Yacht and carrying HRH Prince Edward in a ceremony for the switching on of the new floodlighting there.

In 1992 she was renamed *St Clair II* and her final day in service was 27 February 1992. She was sold to Malaysian owners and renamed *Nusa Penjuang* in June 1992 and was scrapped at Mumbai in 1998.

In January 1978, the roro freighter *Dorset* was chartered and initially relieved *St Ola*, which was receiving attention for a propeller fault, on the Pentland Firth service. She had been built in 1970 as *Donautal* for Hamburg owners at the Rickmers yard in Bremerhaven and served as *Ulster Sportsman* on the Liverpool–Belfast service of the Belfast Steamship Co. from 1974 to spring 1975. She was purchased in May 1978 and renamed *St Magnus*, becoming the sixth vessel of that name in the company's fleet, and operated on the old indirect service that was now running from Aberdeen to Stromness and Lerwick. In July 1980 she called at Sullom Voe on a trial basis, so she could replace *ROF Beaver* if required. She did so for the first time on 21 November 1981. From April 1987, she ran once weekly from Leith to Lerwick, returning to Aberdeen via Stromness, with a second weekly trip from Aberdeen to Stromness, returning from Aberdeen to Leith. From October to December 1987 she used Grangemouth instead of Leith, owing to lock repairs at Leith. She started a Scandinavian service from Aberdeen and Lerwick to Stavanger and Hanstholm in Denmark in September 1989. On 19 December 1989, the Lerwick calls ceased and her final sailing on the route was on 12 April 1990. She had a passenger certificate for fifty and relieved on the Pentland Firth service on occasion. She was moved to Southampton-based services in June 1990 and was then sold. She ran from 1992 to 1996 in the southern Baltic for Polska Zegluga Baltycka as *Parseta* and was then sold to Venezuelan owners Conferrys in 1996, by whom she was renamed *Dona Juana*. She was laid up in 2008 and sank at her anchorage in June 2010.

In 1979 the P&O Ferries logo was added to the superstructure of *St Ola* and the hull of the other vessels and in the following year the hulls became light blue and the P&O flag was painted on the funnel. In 1990 the hull and funnel became dark blue and the 'P&O Ferries' logo on the hull became just 'P&O'.

From the introduction of car ferry services in 1975, the Aberdeen–Lerwick service had only been offered three times weekly, and an additional car ferry was purchased in 1986 to enable daily passenger departures to be given from Aberdeen to Shetland, and also to replace *ROF Beaver*. The northbound Saturday sailings and southbound Friday sailings were routed via Stromness. These weekend round trips were marketed as mini-cruises with a morning ashore at Stromness and a full day at Lerwick the following day, or vice versa. This ferry was *Panther*, which had been built as *Djursland* in 1972 at Helsingør in Denmark for Danish owners. She had operated from 1980 to 1986 from Dover to Boulogne for P&O subsidiary Normandy Ferries. She was renamed *St Sunniva* and rebuilt at the Hall Russell yard to convert her from a day ferry to an overnight ferry; she received an additional 248 berths and entered service on 27 March 1987. During this trip, she was hit by heavy seas and one of her bridge windows was smashed by a large wave – the radio, radar and fire detection equipment was damaged and she had to return to Aberdeen. On 26 April 1988, she sailed on what was supposed to be a mini-cruise to the Glasgow Garden Festival, a visit that had to be extended due to industrial action, with a return to normal service from Stromness on 8 May. In 2002, with the advent of Northlink, she was sold to Dubai owners and renamed *Faye*. She ran from 2003 to 2005 from Port Rashid, Dubai to Umm Qasr, Iraq. She was scrapped at Alang, India in 2005.

In January 1989 the company was renamed P&O Scottish Ferries.

In September 1989, the freight roro *Marino Torre* was chartered for a revived service from Aberdeen to Hanstholm, and in March 1990 she was purchased and renamed *St Rognvald*. She had been built by Orenstein & Koppel at Lübeck in Germany in 1970 as *Rhonetal* and had operated under charter for North Sea Ferries as *Norcape* from 1970 to 1974. She replaced *St Magnus* on the Hanstholm service from 26 April to 26 July 1990, following which the route was discontinued. Shortly after midnight on 5 March 1991, southbound from Lerwick to Aberdeen, her bridge windows were smashed by a large wave and all electrical power was lost, injuring both the master and the mate. Wick lifeboat was launched and two helicopters were scrambled. By 0300 power was re-established but with no steering, and she was going round in circles in winds gusting to a Force 9. At 0515 some steering was available and she went to anchor in Sinclair Bay with the Scapa Flow tug in attendance. At 1800 a tug arrived to tow her to Aberdeen. It was 16 March before she resumed service after repairs. From 1992 some of the calls at Stromness were replaced by ones at Kirkwall. In 1993, she made some midweek sailings for P&O Ferrymasters from Middlesbrough to Gothenburg; in 1994 she was on charter to Color Line in July and August to run weekly from North Shields to Bergen with calls at Stavanger and Haugesund if required. Following the advent of Northlink in 2002, she was chartered to Norse Island Ferries for a brief spell, and was sold to Indian shipbreakers in 2003.

In 1992 both *St Ola* and *St Clair* were replaced with larger ferries. The new *St Ola* was previously *Eckerö* of Eckerö Lines, and had operated from Grisslehamn in Sweden to Eckerd in the Åland Islands since 1982, having been built in 1971 by Meyer Werft at Papenburg on the River Ems in Germany as *Svea Scarlett* for the service from Landskrona to Copenhagen. She entered service on 25 March 1992, on 22 March having made a special 'show the flag' cruise with no passengers aboard round the Orkney mainland with a call at Kirkwall. Following the advent of Northlink in 2002, she was sold to Estonian operator Saaremaa Laevakompanii to serve the route from Kuivatsu to Virtsu on the island of Saaremaa and has spent several spells on charter to the Faeroe Islands. She has been laid up as a reserve ferry since 2010.

The new *St Clair* had been built in 1971 by Schiffbau-Gesellschaft Unterweser at Bremerhaven as *Travemünde* for Moltzau Line's Gedser–Travemünde service. She had been sold in 1980 to a Yugoslavian company as *Njegos*, running across the Adriatic from Bar to Bari, and sold again to Brittany Ferries in 1985, for whom she operated as *Tregastel*. She entered service on 11 March 1992 from Aberdeen to Lerwick. From 14 to 18 May 1992 she made a mini-cruise from Aberdeen to Stavanger. From June to August from 1993 to 1997 she offered a weekend trip from Lerwick to Bergen, as an extension of the Friday departure from Aberdeen, but with only two hours in Bergen from midnight (2300 in later years) to 0200; this was not attractive for mini-cruise passengers. In 1998 and 1999 she made an annual weekend trip at the end of June to the Maløy Festival in Norway. After ten uneventful years serving Lerwick, she was sold in October 2002 to Saudi Arabian owners and renamed *Barakat*, running across the Red Sea from Jeddah to Suakim. In 2011 she was renamed *Noor* and continues to serve on the same route.

The tendering process for the Northern Isles services began in the summer of 1995 and the tender for the ensuing five years was won by P&O Scottish Ferries on 25 July 1997. Expressions of interest for the next tender were invited in the summer of 1998 and this time Caledonian MacBrayne were allowed to tender, which they had not been on the previous occasion. Four companies – P&O Scottish Ferries, Sea Containers, Serco Denholm and Caledonian MacBrayne – were invited to tender in March 2000 and the tender was won by Caledonian MacBrayne. Sea Containers withdrew from the process, Serco Denholm planned to use a single ship and P&O Scottish Ferries planned to use second-hand ships on the Aberdeen routes and re-engine *St Ola*. Caledonian MacBrayne's proposal involved building two new 24-knot ships for the Aberdeen routes and one smaller one for the Pentland Firth service. The new operator was known as Northlink Orkney & Shetland Ferries.

St Clair made her final crossing from Aberdeen to Lerwick, *St Sunniva* from Lerwick to Aberdeen, and *St Ola* from Stromness to Scrabster, on 30 September 2002; *St Rognvald* had been sold two days earlier. And so the curtain came down on the North Company after 212 years.

St Ola after the P&O flag was affixed to the funnel in 1979.

St Ola at Stromness in 1987.

St Ola in 1991 off Scrabster.

St Ola as *St Ola II*, laid up at Leith in 1992.

A stern view of *ROF Beaver* at Aberdeen.

St Clair at Holmsgarth, Lerwick in her 1977–1979 colours.

St Magnus lying off Lerwick in 1982, with *ROF Beaver* and *St Clair* berthed there.

St Magnus in black-hull condition between 1978 and 1979.

St Magnus in 1979.

St Magnus at Aberdeen in 1987.

St Magnus with tanker trailers on deck at Aberdeen 1987.

St Sunniva manoeuvring off the berth at Aberdeen in 1987.

St Sunniva passes under Erskine Bridge on her way to Glasgow Garden Festival, 28 April 1988.

St Sunniva at the Glasgow Garden Festival, May 1988. Note the vintage tram on the riverside tram line in the background.

Marino Torre, soon to become *St Rognvald*, at Stromness in 1989.

St Rognvald at Holmsgarth terminal, Lerwick 1999.

The second car ferry *St Ola*, arriving at Stromness.

St Ola, ex *Eckerö*, in 1992.

The final *St Clair*, ex *Tregastel*, ex *Travemünde*, arriving at Aberdeen.

Chapter 5

Northlink: 2002 to Present Day

Hjaltland off Aberdeen on 14 January 2003 in the original Northlink livery.

Northlink Orkney and Shetland Ferries, a company jointly owned by Caledonian MacBrayne and the Royal Bank of Scotland, commenced operations on 1 October 2002 with the two new Aberdeen ships, *Hjaltland* and *Hrossey*. These had been built by Aker Yards at Rauma in Finland; they are 125 metres long with a capacity of 600 passengers, including 280 berths, increased to 356 in 2007, and 125 cars. A daily service was offered seven days a week from Aberdeen to Lerwick, with calls at a new terminal at Hatston, near Kirkwall, four days a week northbound and three days a week southbound. This reinstated the old indirect service of the North Company.

The new ferry from the Scrabster to Stromness route was named *Hamnavoe*. She came from the same yard and is 112 metres long, with a capacity of 600 day passengers, with 12 cabins, and 110 cars. In recent years, the cabins have been sold on a bed and breakfast basis with passengers sleeping aboard prior to the 0630 sailing from Stromness. The twice-daily return sailings are increased to three times daily from mid-June to the end of August. Due to delays in completing a new pier at Scrabster she did not enter service on the route until 21 April 2003, *Hebridean Isles* of CalMac having filled in on the route since the previous October. After her

2014 refit, *Hamnavoe* was the first of the fleet to carry the new livery of a white hull with the profile of a Viking warrior superimposed in blue towards her stern.

Over the years a number of freight roros have been operated by Northlink, the first being *Hascosay* in 2002. She had been built in 1971 as *Juno* for the Finland Steamship Company, and had changed names and owners several times in the intervening period. She had been on charter to CalMac from 8 April to 27 September 2002 for the Stornoway to Ullapool service. She had berths for twelve passengers and was used in emergency to cover for *Hamnavoe* during her annual overhaul in May 2004. She was sold to Lebanese owners in 2010.

St Rognvald was used for livestock carrying from 7 September to 4 December 2003.

Clare, built as *Wesertal* in 1972, was chartered as an extra freight ferry from June 2004 to 21 December 2010.

The freight roro *Hlldasay*, built in 1999 for Estonian owners ESCO, has been on charter since February 2010, while her sister *Heliar*, built in 1995 for ESCO, has been chartered since January 2011; both have been painted in full Northlink livery and are on charter from Seatruck Ferries.

A new tender was issued from July 2006, two years early, and Caledonian MacBrayne was again the successful bidder, Northlink Ferries Limited being at that time a wholly-owned subsidiary of David MacBrayne Limited.

The subsequent tender was won by the Serco Group and started from 5 July 2012. The change in ownership saw no change to the ships or services.

Hrossey at Aberdeen on 19 September 2014 in the new Northlink livery.

Hamnavoe in her original livery.

Hamnavoe in a storm in the Pentland Firth.

Chapter 6

Competitors and Chartered Vessels

The Isle of Man Steam Packet's first *Ben-my-Chree* of 1845, which ran from Granton to Inverness in 1860 and 1861.

Competitors

Very few operators emerged to compete with the North Company over the years, probably due to the long distances involved.

In 1860 and 1861, the first *Ben-my-Chree* of the Isle of Man Steam Packet Company, built in 1845 by Robert Napier, sailed from Granton to Inverness. She was owned at that time by James Johnson and was sold in 1861 to an Invergordon owner and in the following year to a Liverpool owner.

Cooper & Company of Kirkwall started a service from Kirkwall to Leith in 1898 with George Robertson's steamer *Express* (see below). She was sold to the North Company in 1917 and was replaced that May by *Hebridean*, which had operated from Glasgow to the West Highlands for John McCallum & Co. since she was built at Rutherglen by T. B. Seath & Co. in 1881. She was renamed *Express* and was lost on 9 February 1918 in the Pentland Skerries. In 1920, *Amelia*, built in 1894 by S. McKnight & Co. of Ayr, with a compound engine by Muir & Houston, was purchased. She was sold to the North Company in 1940 along with the business and the service. *Amelia* occasionally carried passengers until 1930.

March 1903 saw the advent of the Edinburgh, Aberdeen & Orkney Shipping Company, which had chartered *Hebridean* from John McCallum & Co. to operate from Leith and Aberdeen to Kirkwall, Stronsay, Sanday and Westray. The North Company and Coopers reduced their rates, but the new operator did not want to engage in a fares war and ceased operating in June of that year.

In June 1903, the Shetland Isles Steam Trading Company Ltd, owned by Sandison's, a firm of general merchants in Yell, started a service from Leith and Aberdeen to Dunrossness, Sandwick, Lerwick, and the North Isles of Shetland with *Mona*, built by Barrow Shipbuilding Co. in 1878 and chartered from the Ayr Steam Shipping Co. In the ensuing winter a more substantial steamer named *Trojan* was chartered in place of *Mona*. At the end of the year, the calls south of Lerwick were reduced to fortnightly. In March 1904, the company purchased its first steamer, *Minnie Hinde* (1891), which had been built by McIlwaine & McColl of Belfast and operated on the Belfast–Whitehaven service, and was renamed *Norseman*. She now operated from Leith, Aberdeen and Lerwick to Whalsay, Yell and Unst in competition with *Earl of Zetland*. By 1907 the company had run out of money and ceased trading: *Norseman* was auctioned off to the Bolivian Government, by whom she was renamed *Explorador*. She sank in Manaus harbour in March 1908.

A firm called Orkney Direct Line, owned by Robert Tulloch of Dundee, was set up in 1938 to run a service from Leith to Kirkwall, Stronsay, Sanday and Westray using the steam coaster *Rota*, built at Grangemouth in 1903. This continued until war broke out; they resumed operation in 1946, but only for a further year.

In December 1984, Norse Atlantic Ferries started a service from Kirkwall to Scalloway with the passenger vessel *Syllingar*, formerly *Scillonian* of the Isles of Scilly Steamship Co., built in 1955 by J. I. Thornycroft & Co. of Southampton. It was not a success and finished on 19 August 1985.

Orcargo ran a freight service from Kirkwall to Invergordon from March 1992 until April 2001 with the freight roro *Contender*, built in 1973 by Ateliers et Chantiers du Havre. The service was latterly subsidised by Orkney Islands Council and ceased in 2001 due to the outbreak of foot and mouth disease, which halted livestock movements.

In 2002 a new operator, Norse Island Ferries, owned by three Shetland haulage companies, Cenargo and Gulf Offshore North Sea, started a freight service from Aberdeen to Lerwick with *Merchant Venture* (1979), which started on 3 September, and *St Rognvald*, which started in October. Initially they took 90 per cent of Northlink's freight trade. *Merchant Venture* was withdrawn in February 2003 after a series of mechanical failures and the company folded on 7 June 2003, due to the bankruptcy of part-owners Cenargo.

Competitors (Pentland Firth)

In 1856, John Stanger, a Stromness boatbuilder, built the small wooden-hulled paddle steamer *Royal Mail* for a new service from Stromness to Scrabster, having obtained the contract for the carriage of the Royal Mail on the route. She continued in service until 1869.

In April 1868, George Robertson placed the wooden paddle steamer *Willngton*, built in Plymouth in 1857, on the Scrabster–Stromness service. She was replaced in September 1868 by the newly built salvage tug *Pera*, and in April 1869 by the new screw steamer *Express*, both of which were built by Readhead Softley at South Shields. *Express* was to have a long life and was eventually purchased by the North Company in 1917.

The railway reached Thurso in 1874, and in 1877 the service was taken over by the Highland Railway Company, which had the screw steamer *John O'Groat* built by Gourlay Bros. of Dundee for the route. She was really too large for the service and in 1879 they were in negotiations to purchase *Express*, but the deal fell through. In March 1881, *John O'Groat* ran aground at Scrabster and was replaced by the former North British Railway paddle steamer *Carham* (1864), which had been on the Strome Ferry–Portree service, but was laid up in Glasgow awaiting sale at the time. *John O'Groat* returned to service after repairs and ran until the North Company took over in July 1882. She was chartered to the North Company from 10 to 26 July 1890, following which she was broken up.

In 1972, a passenger-only service was started from John O'Groats to St Margaret's Hope by Captain William Banks, with a fifty-foot converted air-sea rescue launch named *Pentalina*. Initially, a weekly sailing from St Margaret's Hope to Longhope was also offered, but this only lasted a few weeks. In March 1974 the company Pentland Ferries Ltd was formed to operate the service. May and June 1974 saw three special sailings from St Margaret's Hope to Flotta.

A vessel named *Pentland Spray* offered a summer service from John O'Groats to Burwick from 1973 to 1975. She replaced *Pentland Atom*, which offered a 'sea-taxi' service on the route for Thomas & Bews.

In 1976 she was replaced by the larger *Souter's Lass*, built in 1948 as *Bournemouth Belle* and later named *Weymouth Belle*, and in 1987 by the purpose-built *Pentland Venture* which continues in service today. The sailings are marketed with a connecting bus from Inverness and a bus to Kirkwall or a bus tour of Orkney at the northern end. A day return trip is possible from Inverness to Orkney using this service, now called John O'Groats Ferries.

In 1989, a new company named Orkney Ferries started a car ferry service from Gills Bay to Houton using the newly built *Varagen*, built by Cochrane's of Selby. The first sailing was on 15 August, and she ran until 25 August when she damaged a propeller while leaving Gills Bay and had to sail to Grangemouth for repairs. She returned on 31 August, but no sailings were given until there had been some dredging at Gills Bay. She was running again on 10 and 11 September when she damaged her bow thruster. On 16 September the linkspan at Gills Bay, which was in a very exposed position, was destroyed in a storm and *Varagen* was laid up at Grangemouth. *Varagen* was eventually purchased by the Orkney Islands Shipping Company for service to the North Isles.

On 3 May 2001, a service was again started to Gills Bay, this time from St Margaret's Hope by Pentland Ferries, run by Andrew Banks, son of William Banks, with *Pentalina B*, formerly *Iona* of Caledonian MacBrayne. She was joined by *Claymore*, also previously with Caledonian MacBrayne, in October 2002.

From January 2004, *Pentalina B* was laid up in the winter months. From the end of November 2006, she was chartered to Farmers Ferry to carry cattle from Dover to Dunkirk; this was interrupted in August 2007 by the restrictions on movement of cattle following an outbreak of foot and mouth disease. She sailed for a brief period in early September 2007 from Ipswich as repairs were being made to her berth at Dover. She returned to the Pentland Firth crossing from 21 November 2007 to 6 January 2008. From 10 to 27 December 2008, she was chartered to CalMac for the freight service to Stornoway. The early part of 2009 saw only occasional sailings from Ipswich and Dover to Dunkirk, with much time spent laid up at the French port. She was chartered to CalMac again from 2 to 17 April 2009 for the Kennacraig–Port Askaig service, mainly with freight traffic. She was sold in January 2010 to owners in the Cape Verde Islands, where she operated carrying machinery and heavy loads between the islands. She ran aground in the bay of Moia-Moia on the island of Santiago in June 2014 while en route from the island of Boa Vista to Praia. A basic roadway was constructed to enable the vehicles on board to disembark, and it was uncertain if she would be salvaged.

In August 2002, *Claymore* was purchased by Pentland Ferries and she operated from St Margaret's Hope to Invergordon from 11 to 29 November 2002. She was then laid up, being reactivated for the Gills Bay service from 7 March to 3 April 2003 and again from 1 November 2003 to 3 June 2004, initially on a twelve-passenger basis but with a winter certificate for seventy-one and summer for 250 from 19 January 2004. She was on the route again from 10 November 2004 to April 2005 and for a similar period in subsequent winters. From June to October 2006 she was on charter to Farmers Ferry Ltd for livestock sailings from Dover to Boulogne and Dunkirk. In 2007 she remained on the Pentland Firth service until 21 November. In her overhaul that month she lost her hoist and side ramps and her hull was painted red. She was back in service again from 11 January 2008 to 29 March 2009, with spells off for overhaul in December 2008 and from 29 January to 12 February 2009. At the end of March 2009 she was sold to the Danish company CT Offshore, renamed *Sia*, and converted to be used as a cable layer. The addition of four bow thrusters made her extremely manoeuvrable in her new role. She is now used for laying cables for wind farms in the North Sea.

Both of these vessels were replaced by the Philippine-built catamaran *Pentalina*, who had a long delivery voyage from the Philippines. She left the Philipines on 25 July 2008, but was so dogged by delays that she did not arrive at St Margaret's Hope until 22 December. Her first voyage was on 23 December 2008, although it was 5 February 2009 until she received her passenger certificate and could carry more than twelve passengers.

In February 2015, Pentland Ferries purchased the CalMac ferry *Saturn* (1977), to be used in connection with the building of windfarms in Orkney and as a freight vessel on the route. She was moved from her lay-up berth at Rosneath in the Gareloch to the Garvel dry dock in Greenock, and then to the James Watt dock in mid-March where she was repainted with a red hull and red funnels like Claymore. She is to be renamed, but the new name is not known at the time of writing.

A model of Stanger's wooden paddler *Royal Mail*, which ran from Stromness to Scrabster from 1856 to 1869.

George Roberson's *Express*, built in 1869 for the Pentland Forth service, which was purchased by the North Company in 1917 and was lost in April of that year.

Chieftain's Bride, which ran to the North Isles of Shetland from 1868 to 1877.

Norseman (1891), which ran from Leith and Aberdeen to the North Isles of Shetland from 1904 to 1907, seen here dressed overall at Lerwick.

Cooper & Co.'s cargo steamer *Amelia* at Leith in the 1930s.

Pentland Venture at John O'Groats in 1989.

Sovereign (1836) entering Aberdeen Harbour.

St Magnus departing Aberdeen around 1965 or 1966.

St Ola at Stromness in summer 1968.

A postcard view of the car ferry *St Ola* in her original North Company colours.

ROF Beaver at Aberdeen, 1986.

The car ferry *St Clair* with a black hull and P&O Ferries logo, between 1977 and 1979, in the Sound of Bressay.

St Sunniva at Stromness on one of her weekend mini-cruises in 1999.

St Clair at Aberdeen in 2001.

A closer view of the Viking warrior logo on *Hrossey*.

Hamnavoe and *St Clair* at Leith in 2002, when the former was laid up there awaiting completion of pier works at Scrabster.

The launch of *Pentalina* at John O'Groats in the early seventies, before the harbour was enlarged.

Souters Lass, lying at Scrabster 1987.

The coaster *Rosemarkie*, chartered in 1976 for the cargo service.

The livestock carrier *Shorthorn Express* departs Aberdeen in 1985.

Earl Sigurd off Hatston in the twilight of her career, 1968.

The two 1990 car ferries *Earl Sigurd* and *Earl Thorfinn* berthed at Kirkwall early in their careers.

Varagen in Orkney Ferries livery after 1995.

Klydon, a former Danish coaster that served the Kirkwall to Shapinsay service from 1963 to 1969.

The car ferry *Shapinsay* at Kirkwall, with *Clytus* moored to the left.

Clytus on the Shapinsay service in 1982.

Hoy Head at Stromness in 1968.

Hendra in 1990.

The charter *Hebridean Isles* at Scrabster on 1 October 2002, with the pier there being extended to accommodate *Hamnavoe*.

The chartered *Hebridean Isles* and *Hamnavoe* at Stromness on 12 April 2003.

Pentalina B departs St Margaret's Hope while *Claymore* is at the berth on 23 October 2002.

Claymore in red-hulled condition between November 2007 and March 2009 at Gills Bay.

Hrossey in the Sound of Bressay on 14 January 2003 in the original Northlink livery.

The current, second, *Filla* at Out Skerries.

Linga of 2002.

Hildasay departing from Aberdeen. (Colin J. Smith)

Helliar departing Aberdeen. (Colin J. Smith)

Pentalina departing St Margaret's Hope, seen from Hoxa Head. (Colin J. Smith)

Orcargo's *Contender* at Scrabster, with *St Ola* departing and *Varagen* lying behind her.

North Company Chartered Vessels

The North Company relied heavily on chartered vessels at three periods in its history: the Second World War, when cargo steamers were chartered to meet the demand for freight transport serving the naval and military bases in the islands; the latter part of the twentieth century, when the demand in autumn for livestock transport led to the charter of specialised livestock carriers; and the car ferry era, when various CalMac ferries were chartered to provide the Pentland Firth service during the overhaul of the third and fourth *St Ola*'s and, in the Northlink era, *Hamnavoe*.

In 1857 and 1858, three steamers were chartered from the Aberdeen Steam Navigation Co. to fill a gap after the loss of *Queen* and *Duke of Richmond*. These were the wooden-hulled paddle steamer *Commodore*, built in 1838 by John Wood at Port Glasgow for G. & J. Burns and purchased by the Aberdeen company in 1855; the iron-hulled paddle steamer *City of Aberdeen* (1835), built by Scotts at Greenock, both of which operated in both years, and the screw *Duke of Rothesay* (1857), built by Denny of Dumbarton, chartered in 1858 only.

In 1863, following the loss of *Hamburg* in the previous year, the wooden-hulled paddle steamer *Dundee* (1834), built by John Wood at Port Glasgow with engines by Robert Napier, was chartered from the Dundee, Perth & London Company to run to Wick in April and to Lerwick in May.

In 1867, following the loss of *Prince Consort*, *Princess Alice* of the Aberdeen & Newcastle Shipping Co., built in 1843 by Tod & McGregor, was chartered, as was *Dundee* again. The screw steamer *Oscar* (1861), of the London & Edinburgh Shipping Company, built by John Pile & Co. of West Hartlepool, was also chartered.

Following the sale of *St Olaf* to Canada in 1890, a series of chartered vessels maintained the Pentland Firth service until *St Ola* was built in 1892. These were: *John O'Groat*, of McCallum & Co., which had been built for the Highland Railway Company's service on the route in 1877 (see previous chapter) and was only on charter from 10 to 26 July 1890, following which she was broken up; *Argyll* (1886) of the Argyll Steamship Co., normally on the Glasgow–Stranraer service, and *Express* (1869), from 12 October 1890 to 30 August 1891, which had operated on the route from building until it was taken over by the Highland Railway in 1877. *Argyll* was again chartered in the 1891/1892 winter for the direct service from Aberdeen to Lerwick.

The cargo steamer *Nigel* (1886), built by Scotts of Bowling with machinery by Muir & Houston, was chartered from A. F. Blackwater of Glasgow from 1891 to 1892 for the direct service, carrying mails and cargo only.

In 1900, following the loss of the first *St Rognvald*, *City of Aberdeen* (1873), built by Cunliffe & Dunlop of Port Glasgow, was chartered from the Aberdeen Steam Navigation Co. for the weekend service.

During the years of the Second World War, control of the shipping services was taken over by the Ministry of War Transport. Vessels were allocated as necessary to the routes, not all being formally chartered by the North Company.

In August 1939, the steam coaster *Naivedale* (1906), built by Ailsa Shipbuilding Co. at Ayr, was chartered for a service from Leith to Lyness and continued on charter, serving on the Wick and Scrabster service and elsewhere when required. She was chartered again from April to June 1946. She was joined in September by the similar *Rimsdale* (1923), built by Hanson Shipbuilding at Bideford for Cardiff owners as *Wheathill*. *Berriedale* (1922), built by John Chambers Ltd at Lowestoft, joined the chartered cargo fleet in autumn 1940. *Kildrummy* (1924), of the Dundee, Perth & London Co., built by Hall Russell, was chartered for a single trip in August 1940 and *Blyth* (1931), built by Cammell Laird, from the Goole Fleet of Associated Humber Lines, was allocated by the Ministry of War Transport from May to August 1941.

Morialta, a new motor vessel which had been under construction at the Caledon yard at Dundee for the Adelaide Steamship Co. in Australia, was requisitioned by the Admiralty and was managed by the North Company from October 1940. She joined *St Ninian* in running from Scrabster to the depot ship HMS *Dunluce Castle*, moored in Scapa Flow. HMS *Dunluce Castle*, moored in Scapa Flow, to Scrabster. On 8 June 1942, she carried King George VI whilst he was reviewing the fleet. She moved away in August 1943 and was transferred to Mediterranean service, not being delivered to her owners until 1946.

The Norwegian coastal steamer *Galtesund*, which was had been hijacked by her crew in March 1942 and sailed from Nazi-occupied Norway to Aberdeen, ran from Aberdeen to Kirkwall and Scapa Flow from August to October 1942 for the North Company.

The Faeroese steamer *Tjaldur*, built in Copenhagen in 1916, was managed by the North Company from June 1943, and replaced *Morialta* in August of that year. Some twenty-one vessels operated on the Pentland Firth crossing during the Second World War, including the Great Western Railway's Plymouth tenders *Sir Richard Grenville* and *Sir John Hawkins* and the Red Funnel tender *Calshot*.

Three so-far unidentified General Steam Navigation Company cargo vessels were allocated to the North Company during the war years.

Two further steamers were allocated to the North Company on 16 December 1944, *Nova* (1925) of the Bergen Steamship Company, built at Le Trait in France, which operated from Aberdeen to the Faeroes and to Lerwick until September 1945, and *Lochnagar* (1906) of the Aberdeen Steam Navigation Co., which operated from Aberdeen to Lerwick until January 1946.

The cargo motor vessel *Edina* (1939) of James Currie & Co. of Leith, which had been built by Henry Robb Ltd at Leith, was chartered from March to June 1946.

In February 1968, *Lairdscrest* was transferred from Burns Laird Lines to cover for an extended refit of *Earl of Zetland*. She replaced *St Clement* on the Leith–Kirkwall–Stromness cargo service, which herself replaced *St Ola*, which replaced the *Earl*.

In the second half of 1974, the GSN coaster *Ortolan* (1964), built by John Lewis & Sons Ltd. at Torry, Aberdeen, was transferred to the North Company to provide a freight service on the Aberdeen–Lerwick route. Her use continued into 1975 and 1976, being used on oil-related work, making calls at Leith, Inverkeithing, Dundee, Peterhead, Flotta, Lyness, Kirkwall, Sandwick and Sullom Voe. Much of this was in connection with the construction of facilities to deal with the new North Sea Oil bonanza, particularly at Flotta and Sullom Voe. In September 1977, she was on the Aberdeen–Kirkwall cargo service while *St Rognvald* was on livestock sailings.

Her sister *Oriole* (1963), also built by Lewis, was used around 1975 on North Company services from Aberdeen to Kirkwall and Lerwick, while *Petrel* (1965), built by J. Bolson & Sons Ltd at Poole, ownership of which had been transferred to P&O Ferries (General European) in April 1976, was used on occasion in 1976 and 1977.

From late January 1975 until 30 January 1976, the Zetland County Council car ferry *Grima* was chartered for a twice-weekly service from Lerwick to Symbister on Whalsay, the terminals at Symbister and at Laxo on the mainland not yet having been completed and *Earl of Zetland* making her final voyage for the company on 21 February 1975.

From 3 to 18 November 1975, *Clansman* (1964), of Caledonian MacBrayne, relieved *St Ola* for overhaul on the Scrabster–Stromness service, and did so every year until 1982/83.

The former Dutch coaster *Rosemarkie* (1957) of W. N. Lindsay of Leith was also chartered in 1976 for the cargo service.

Lairdsfox (1952), of Burns Laird Lines, was chartered in June 1977 and the Danish coaster *Bussard* (1961) was chartered in October 1977 to replace *Ortolan* on the Kirkwall cargo service.

Specialist livestock carriers were chartered in annually from 1977 onwards following the demise of the cargo service, starting with *Angus Express* (1950) from 17 September to 28 November 1977. They generally operated from Kirkwall and Lerwick to Aberdeen, although there were also some sailings from Baltasound from 1983 to 1991, ceasing because of the condition of the pier there. Unusual sailings included Stromness–Scrabster on 13 October 1985; Baltasound–Invergordon in 1987 and Lyness–Scrabster on 7 October 1989, all by *Shorthorn Express*. In 1988, a couple of calls were made at Peterhead, one north- and one south-bound.

The livestock carriers chartered were (from 2002 by Northlink):

Angus Express (1950)	1977	1980				
Shorthorn Express (1957)	1980	1982-1990				
Frisian Express (1957)	1981	1982-1984				
Lincoln Express (1953)	1981					
Irish Rose (1965)	1984	1986	1988	1993	1994	1996-8
Irish Provider (1964)	1985	1987	1989	1990	1992	1995
Angus Express (1967)	1991-2001					
Caroline (1993)	2002					
Buffalo Express (1983)	2002	2007	+3 more			
Zebu Express (1984)	2003	2005				

From 2008, special livestock containers were used on the car deck to avoid the need to charter dedicated livestock carriers.

The Norwegian freight roro *Nornan Fjord* (1974), built by Kremer at Elmshorn in Germany, was used to bring in animal feedstuffs to the islands in 1978. In February of the following year, after she had been sold to James Fisher of Barrow in Furness and renamed *Sea Fisher*, she was chartered to relieve *St Magnus* for overhaul. The West Germen roro *Condor* (1972) was also chartered from 5 to 10 February 1979, and was followed by the Norwegian *Austri* (1969) from 10 to 24 February.

The German roro *Transit* (1972) was chartered in May/June 1980 to replace *ROF Beaver* for overhaul.

In February 1982, the Faroese ferry *Smyril*, ex *Morten Mols* (1969), built at Aalborg Værft in Denmark, was chartered to relieve *St Magnus* while she was relieving *St Clair* and during her own overhaul and then that of *St Ola*. She replaced *St Clair* in October 1982, and again in 1984 from 19 February to 7 April, and from 29 September to 12 October 1989 relieved *St Magnus* on the Hanstholm service. She was on charter again from 6 to 14 March 1991 after *St Rognvald*'s storm damage (see Chapter 4), and also to cover for *St Clair* being away for overhaul.

The Orkney Islands Shipping Company's *Orcadia* was chartered to replace *St Ola* during her repair after her engine room fire from 2 to 27 November 1982 after *Smyril* had to return to the Faeroes. She sailed on a twice-weekly service from Kirkwall to Scrabster, rather than from Stromness, on days she would normally have been idle, although a number of sailings went to Wick due to weather and tidal conditions rather than Scrabster. *Clansman* was called in at the end of November, but had to rerun to the west coast and *Orcadia* had another spell on the route, sailing twice weekly in January 1983. *St Magnus* and *ROF Beaver* took the freight service from Scrabster during these periods. From 31 May to 6 September 1986, *Orcadia* was chartered to operate an inter-island service from Kirkwall to Scalloway, sailing north on a Saturday and back south on a Sunday, following the demise of the service provided by *Syllingar*. On occasion she was diverted to Lerwick.

From 20 February to 6 March 1983, *Penn ar Bed* (1974) of Brittany Ferries relieved *St Clair* for overhaul. She only had a passenger certificate for fifty compared to the 700 of *St Clair*, probably the reason that the charter was not repeated.

The cargo roro *Juniper* (1977) was chartered from late July to early December 1989.

The Aberdeen Steam Navigation Co.'s *City of Aberdeen* (1835), chartered in 1857 and 1858.

Perth (1834), the sister of the Dundee, Perth & London Shipping Company's *Dundee*, which was chartered in 1863 after the loss of *Hamburg*.

The Argyll SS Co.'s *Argyll*, chartered in the 1891/1892 winter on the 'direct' route from Aberdeen to Lerwick. She had been built in 1886 by Robert Duncan & Co. of Glasgow, and normally ran from Glasgow to Campbeltown and Stranraer. She was wrecked at Milleur Point at the entrance to Loch Ryan, on 17 September 1893.

The steam coaster *Naviedale*, chartered from 1939, through the war years and in 1946.

The steam coaster *Rimsdale*, chartered from September 1939.

The Dundee, Perth & London's steamer *Kildrummy*, chartered for a single trip in August 1940.

Aire, sister of *Blyth*, which was allocated to the North Company by the Ministry of War Transport from May to August 1941.

Morialta, newly built for New Zealand owners by Caledon in Dundee, and operated from Scrabster to HMS *Dunluce Castle* from October 1940 to August 1943.

The Faeroese steamer *Tjaldur* of 1916, managed by the North Company from 1943 to the end of the war.

The Plymouth tender *Sir Richard Grenville*, used on the Pentland Forth service during the 1939–1945 war.

The Norwegian coastal steamer *Galtesund*, operated by the North Company in 1942.

S.S. "LOCHNAGAR."

The fine Passenger Steamers of The Aberdeen Steam Navigation Company Limited sailing between London and Aberdeen twice weekly.

COPYRIGHT,
ROBERTSON. PHOTO.
ABERDEEN.

The Aberdeen Steam Navigation Company's *Lochnagar* of 1906, which ran from Aberdeen to Lerwick from December 1944 until January 1946.

Burns Laird's cargo vessel *Lairdscrest*, which was transferred within the P&O Group in early 1968 for two-and-a-half round trips from Leith to Kirkwall and Stromness to cover the overhaul period.

Clansman, chartered for the Pentland Firth service during *St Ola*'s overhaul between 1975 and 1982, at Scrabster.

The GSN Co.'s *Ortolan*, chartered from 1974 to 1976.

The General Steam Navigation Co.'s *Petrel*, used at times in 1976 and 1977, immediately prior to the introduction of roro freight services.

Burns Laird's *Lairdsfox*, transferred to the North Company for a spell in 1977.

Livestock carrier *Angus Express* (1967), chartered every year from 1991 to 2001.

The livestock carrier *Frisian Express* on the River Clyde passes a partially completed Erskine Bridge around 1969.

The livestock carrier *Irish Rose*.

Livestock carrier *Lidrott* (1964), formerly *Irish Provider*, chartered between 1985 and 1995.

The Faroese car ferry *Smyril*, chartered to P&O Ferries in the 1980s.

Orcadia at sea in 1982 while on charter to the North Company, replacing *St Ola*.

Orcadia at Scrabster while on charter to the North Company in November 1982.

Chapter 7

Orkney Inter-Island Steamers and Ferries

The long-serving North Isles steamer *Orcadia*, of 1868.

North Isles

The first steamer to serve the North Isles of Orkney was the first *Orcadia*, operated by George Robertson. She was a wooden-hulled screw steamer, formerly named *Aberlleveny Quarry Maid* and built in 1859 by Lewis of Aberdovey for owners in Aberystwyth. She operated in Orkney from 1865 to 1868. She entered service on 29 March 1865 and was joined in early May by a paddle steamer named *Rover*, which appears to have been chartered.

By 1868, a larger steamer was required and the Orkney Steam Navigation Company was founded with George Robertson as manager. A new steamer, also named *Orcadia*, was built by Readhead Softley & Co. of South Shields. She served the North Isles of Stronsay, Eday, Sanday, and Westray; in 1884 she was lengthened by 20 feet and re-engined. She operated until 1931 and was then used as a coal hulk at Stronsay until scrapped in 1934.

In 1892 a steamer named *Fawn* was purchased by the Orkney Steam Navigation Company to serve Rousay. She had been built in Kiel, Germany in 1869 and remained in service until 1917. She had previously been owned by the New Southampton Steam Towing Co. Ltd. and used as a tug.

She was replaced on the Rousay service by the *Countess of Bantry* in 1919. She had been built in 1884 by Workman Clark at Belfast, with engines by William Kemp of Glasgow, to run from Bantry to Castletownbere, and had been purchased in 1901 by Alexander Paterson for excursions out of Oban. She served Rousay until 1928 and was scrapped in 1934.

In 1926, the triple-expansion engined steamer *Earl Thorfinn* was built by Hall Russell for the North Isles service to replace *Orcadia*, and she was joined by a sister, *Earl Sigurd*, in 1931. *Earl Thorfinn* remained in service until 1963 and *Earl Sigurd* until 1969, by which time she was the last commercially operated coal-fired screw steamer in the UK. At some stage, probably in the thirties, calls were added at Papa Westray and North Ronaldsay. North Ronaldsay still only gets a sailing once a week in the winter months and twice in the summer.

On 1 January 1962, the Orkney Steam Navigation Co. was renamed Orkney Islands Shipping Co. Later that year, the motor vessel *Orcadia*, built by Hall Russell, entered service to replace *Earl Thorfinn*. She normally offered a round trip to the islands on a Monday and Friday, and a two-day trip, overnighting at Westray, on a Wednesday. In addition to her scheduled service, she operated occasional excursions from the islands to Kirkwall, an annual trip (sometimes two) from Kirkwall to Fair Isle and, on 8–9 July 1972 and 3–4 August 1974, a two-day excursion from Kirkwall to Lerwick for the inter-island football and hockey matches. She remained in service until 1990, her final sailing being on 24 August 1990, and, after a spell laid up at Leith, was sold to Caribbean owners in 1994 and refitted in Florida. She was renamed *Louisa* in 1999. In 2004 she was back across the Atlantic at El Puerto de Santa Maria, near Cadiz. She was raided by the Spanish Civil Guard in 2006, and was found to be operated by an armed gang who were engaged in plundering archaeological artefacts from the seabed. Police found rifles, ammunition and remains of seventeenth- to eighteenth-century cannon balls from the Battle of Trafalgar. She was seized by the Spanish authorities and, as far as it is known, remains laid up and under arrest there to this day.

In 1969, a twelve-passenger engines-aft cargo ship, *Islander*, was built for the North Isles service by J. Lewis & Co., of Aberdeen, entering service on 7 July of that year and replacing *Earl Sigurd*. On 2 July 1976, she ran aground on Vasa Skerry to the west of Shapinsay, and had to be towed into Kirkwall by *Clytus*. She remained in service until 23 August 1991, and was sold in 1993 to Honduras owners who renamed her *Mary Pau*.

Watchful was chartered from Bremner & Co. to cover for *Islander* during her overhaul period in 1972 and to operate part of her schedule.

It was planned that CalMac's *Bute* visit the North Isles in February 1978 to see if that type of vessel could operate to the existing terminals but that visit did not materialise.

The small passenger vessel *Golden Mariana*, built in 1973 at Bideford, entered service in 1986, having previously been a tourist boat at Ullapool and then owned by Pentland Ferries. She operated in that year on behalf of Orkney Islands Council, on a Sunday service to Shapinsay, and also operated in 1987 to Shapinsay, with a Balfour

Castle cruise on Wednesdays and on summer-day excursions from Kirkwall to the North Isles. In July and August 1990, she operated a twice-weekly service to Eday, as *Orcadia* and *Earl Thorfinn* were unable to call there due to reconstruction work on the pier. She relieved *Eynhallow* and *Shapinsay* for overhaul from late spring 1991. In summer 1992, she operated services from Kirkwall to the North Isles. Since 1993 she has been on a summer shuttle service from Pierowall, Westray, to Papa Westray.

On 1 April 1987, Orkney Islands Shipping Co. was taken over by Orkney Islands Council.

In 1990, the car ferry came to the North Isles with the introduction of a new *Earl Thorfinn* and *Earl Sigurd*, both built by James Miller at St Monans, with hulls by McTay Marine at Bromborough in the Wirral, and entering service in August and November of that year respectively. On 30 August 1991, they were joined by *Varagen*, previously on a brief spell for the abortive Gills Bay–Houton service, which mainly served Eday and Stronsay up to 1993. Initially using crane loading, roro service was established to Eday and Stronsay in July 1991, Sanday and Rapness in Westray, replacing the previous call at Pierowall, followed in October and November 1992 respectively; vehicles to North Ronaldsay and Papa Westray are still crane-loaded to this day. *Varagen*, not having a crane, does not serve either of these islands.

In 1995 the company was renamed Orkney Ferries Ltd.

Shapinsay

The small steamer *Iona* operated as a mail steamer from Kirkwall to Shapinsay for over seventy years, beginning in 1893, when she was built locally by T. B. Stevenson, up to November 1964, when she sank in a storm at Shapinsay Pier. She was originally owned by John Reid and was taken over in 1914 by William Dennisson, both being from Shapinsay. She was dieselised in 1949.

Iona was replaced by *Klydon*, a diesel coaster built in Cologne in 1963. In April 1969 she was on charter to Alginate Industries Ltd and ran aground at Tarbert, Harris, and was sold to her charterers after she was salvaged, being renamed *Alga*. She carried cargoes of seaweed around the Western Isles for twenty years or more, but her ultimate fate is unknown to the author.

The motor launches *Orana* and *Sheena* were operated by John Nicholson from Kirkwall to Shapinsay and were chartered to Dennisson when *Klydon* was not available. They operated from Kirkwall to Balfour from 1969 until *Clytus* entered service in 1970.

The Danish coaster *Helle Rask* was chartered for cargo to Shapinsay from the time of the loss of *Klydon* until Dennison's gave up the service in December 1969.

The Shapinsay service was taken over by the Orkney Islands Shipping Company in 1970. After initially using *Watchful* (chartered from Bremners), they purchased the former Clyde pilot cutter *Gantock,* which was built by Hugh MacLean at Renfrew in 1944 with Gardner engines, and was renamed *Clytus. Islander* provided the cargo service. In June 1976, *Sheena*, owned by A. Nicolson, and *Shalder*, owned by Mansie Flaws of Wyre, were chartered for the service for a week or so after *Clytus* had broken down. A vessel named *Jennie Lee* was chartered in May 1986 to relieve on a Wednesday when *Clytus* was away for overhaul and relief vessel *Lyrawa Bay* was also relieving *Islander. Clytus* served there until she was withdrawn in May 1989, when she was sold to a diving company.

On 29 July 1989, the purpose-built landing-craft style car ferry *Shapinsay*, built at Buckie by Jones Buckie Shipyard Co., with the hull constructed by Yorkshire Drydock Co. of Hull, entered service on the Kirkwall–Shapinsay route. She is still in service there, sailing every 90 to 105 minutes throughout the day. She was lengthened by 9 metres and re-engined at Macduff in 2011. In May 1990, she was relieved for overhaul by *Canna*, chartered from Caledonian MacBrayne.

Rousay, Wyre and Egilsay

The wooden-hulled steamer *Lizzie Burroughs* was built for the Rousay, Evie & Rendall Steam Navigation Company in 1879 at Leith for the service from Kirkwall to Egilsay, Wyre and Rousay. Calls were made on Mondays and Tuesdays at Rendall Point (Mainland), Gairsay, Tingwall (Mainland), Evie (Mainland), Hullion (Rousay), Veira (Wyre), Trumland (Rousay), Egilsay and Sourin (Rousay). On Mondays she started the day at Sourin and made a single journey to Kirkwall, returning on Tuesdays. On Wednesdays, Thursdays and Saturdays she started from Trumland in the morning and returned from Kirkwall in the afternoon. A call was also made at Aikerness on the mainland on Wednesdays and Saturdays. The Thursday sailing only called at Egilsay and Wyre and there were no regular sailings on Fridays or Sundays. The company was wound up and *Lizzie Burroughs* sold in 1892. She was sold to Robert Garden of Kirkwall and renamed *Aberdeen*. She was then used on cargo work, serving her owners' shops in Sutherland and operating on various Orkney routes as a relief steamer. Her engines were removed in 1897 and she was sold to Wick owners in 1903.

Rousay, Egilsay and Wyre were served by the Orkney Steam Navigation Co.'s *Fawn* from 1892 onwards and then by the North Isles steamers until August 1987 when the landing-craft style ferry *Eynhallow*, built at Bristol, entered service for the Orkney Islands Shipping Company from Tingwall to Rousay, Wyre and Egilsay. She was lengthened by 5 metres in 1991 and continues on the route at the time of writing.

The steamer *Earl Thorfinn* of 1926.

Earl Sigurd departing Kirkwall, post-war.

Earl Sigurd at her berth at North Ronaldsay in 1968.

Orcadia in 1968.

The North Isles before the car ferry! *Orcadia* crane-loading a car in 1982.

A van being crane-loaded on *Orcadia* at Kirkwall, 1982.

Orcadia in her present condition, laid up near Cadiz under the name *Louisa*.

The North Isles cargo vessel *Islander* in 1982.

Islander arriving at Kirkwall in 1982.

Earl Sigurd at Kirkwall in 1990, or early 1991.

Earl Thorfinn at Kirkwall in 1999, with *Clytus* just off the pier.

The Shapinsay steamer *Iona*, which was in service from 1893 to 1964.

Klydon under overhaul, hauled up on land.

Shapinsay ferry *Clytus*, the former Clyde pilot boat *Gantock*, in 1982.

Clytus at Kirkwall in 1999, with the upperworks of *Thorsvoe* on the other side of the quay.

The Rousay, Egilsay and Wyre steamer *Fawn*, which served the islands from 1892 until 1917.

Countess of Bantry at Oban in a pre-1914 view with *Chevalier*.

Countess of Bantry at Oban, seen in a photograph attached to her sale notice in 1919.

The current Rousay, Egilsay and Wyre car ferry, *Eynhallow*, at Rousay on 21 June 1994.

The South Isles

The steamer *Saga* was built in Stromness in 1893 for the Stromness–Longhope service for the newly formed South Isles Steam Packet Co. She was sold in August 1895 to the Cromarty Steamship Co. for service from Cromarty to Invergordon. She was purchased by the Admiralty in the First World War and was used in the Dardanelles campaign. She was sold back to Firth of Clyde owners in the early 1920s and was used to carry scrap metal. Latterly, she was laid up at Port Bannatyne cargo pier for a number of years, and was scrapped *in situ* in 1939.

Robert Garden, a Kirkwall merchant, started a service from Scapa Pier to the South Isles in 1889 with the steamer *Endeavour*, which had been built in Leith in 1884. A diesel engine was fitted in her in 1913 and she remained in service until 1928, being scrapped in 1930. She was really a floating shop but carried some passengers. Post 1918, she served the North Isles as a shop and was based at Papa Westray.

Robert Garden introduced the steamer *Hoy Head*, built by T. B. Seath at Rutherglen, in 1896. She ran from Stromness to Graemsay, Longhope and Flotta on four days a week, with a weekly run to St Margaret's Hope and Scapa after 1918 to coincide with market day in Kirkwall. In 1919, the Stromness & South Isles Steam Packet Co. took over the steamer and her service, followed in 1921 by Swanson & Towers and in 1938 by Bremner & Co. She lasted until scrapped in 1956.

Bremner & Co. were very busy during the war years and purchased two steam drifters: *Premier*, built in 1908 by Beeching Brothers of Great Yarmouth, with machinery by Crabtree & Co., and *Pride o' Fife*, built in 1907 by William Geddes at Port Gordon, with machinery by John Lewis of Aberdeen, in 1940. The latter was broken up in 1945 and *Premier* was sold in 1945 and broken up in 1946.

In 1943, the steam coaster *Wisbech*, built in 1916 by W. H. Warren at New Holland on the Humber, was purchased. She was sold at the end of 1952 and broken up in 1960.

1947 saw the purchase of another steam coaster, *Cushag*, built in 1908 as *Ardnagrena* for County Antrim owners by George Brown at Greenock, with engines by Renfrew Brothers of Irvine. She had had a peripatetic history, including a spell from 1920 to 1943 operating for the Isle of Man Steam Packet Co. She was sold in 1954 and broken up in 1957.

In 1947 the South Isles got their own *Orcadia*, built in 1905 by Cox & Co. at Falmouth in 1905. She took over the South Isles run from *Hoy Head*, which was then placed in reserve. She had been built as the Admiralty steam tender *Playfair*, serving Inchkeith in the Firth of Forth. She was sold in 1958 for a proposed conversion to a fishing vessel, but that proved impracticable and she was scrapped.

In 1952, another steam coaster was purchased by Bremner & Co.: *Orkney Trader*, built in 1908 by the Dublin Dockyard Company, with machinery by Ross & Duncan. She was sold for breaking up in 1959.

The first *Orkney Dawn* joined Bremner's fleet in 1953. She was another steam coaster, built in 1921 by Cook, Welton & Gemmell at Beverley, with an engine by C. D. Holmes of Hull, and was sold in 1955 and broken up two years later. She was replaced in 1955 by the second *Orkney Dawn*, a similar vessel which had been built in 1916 by Cochrane & Sons of Selby, with machinery by Hall Russell, which was sold two years later for scrapping.

Another steam coaster, *Finvoy*, was purchased in 1957. She had been built in 1924 by Forth Shipbuilding & Engineering at Alloa for Belfast owners. On her third voyage her furnace crown burnt out when on a voyage from the Humber to Kirkwall with barley. She was towed to Kirkwall and then to Aberdeen for repairs and lay there for some months due to a strike in the yard; she was sold for breaking up at Irvine in November 1958.

These coasters were mainly used for conveying the sections of dismantled military huts from Orkney back to mainland Britain, with coal and other bulk cargoes being carried northbound.

In 1958, a former MFV, built in 1955 by G. Thomson at Buckie, with machinery by Norris, Henty & Gardner of Manchester, was purchased by the Secretary of State for Scotland. She named *Hoy Head* and chartered to Bremner & Co. to replace *Orcadia* on the mail run from Stromness and Scapa Pier to Longhope and Flotta. She was spare vessel after the introduction of *Lyrawa Bay* in 1976 and remained in the fleet until 1986, then being sold to Viking Sea Taxis of Shetland and renamed *Zenobia* to tender to the 'Klonyker' eastern bloc fish factory ships, and was later in use as a workboat. She was moved to the Clyde and used as a motor yacht. She was stranded while returning to Irvine in 2012 and, as far as it is known, the wreck remains there.

A second MFV, built in 1944 by Nobles of Girvan with Mirrlees Blackstone engines, was purchased in 1961 and renamed *Watchful*. She mainly operated a second summer service to the South Isles and was withdrawn from service and sold in June 1976.

Bremner & Company was taken over by the Orkney Islands Shipping Company on 1 April 1974.

The Admiralty ran MFV *1187* on a service from Lyness to Houton from the outbreak of war in 1939 until May 1956.

From 1921 to 1928, *Countess Cadogan*, which had been built in 1897 by J. McArthur & Co. in Paisley for service on the Shannon, operated a competing service from Stromness to Longhope and Flotta for Captain Robert Arcus, with a St Margaret's Hope call added on Mondays from March 1922. On the death of Captain Arcus, in 1924 the steamer was taken over by James Sutherland. She was broken up in 1932.

In 1898, the steamer *Cormorant*, built in Berwick in 1885, was purchased by Robert Garden. She served his shops on the west coast of Sutherland as far south as Loch Broom. She was sold in 1934 to John R. Laird of Burray for use as a relief steamer to *Sutors* and was broken up in 1938.

Sutors, built in Inverness in 1913, was purchased in 1925 by Andrew Laird of Burray. She ran from Burray to Scapa Pier, Kirkwall on Mondays and to St Margaret's Hope on Thursdays to connect with the weekly call of the North Company steamer. She remained in service until 1938.

In 1938, the former Girvan–Ailsa Crag steamer *Ailsa*, built at the Ailsa yard in Troon in 1906, was purchased by John R. Laird. She had been operating on the Cromarty Firth since 1924. She operated until taken over by the Admiralty in 1943 and was later used in the Normandy landings.

The motor boat *Hoxa Head*, owned by John McBeath, tendered to *St Ola* at St Margaret's Hope from 1912, taking goods and passengers to South Ronaldsay and Burray. She also ran weekly on Mondays to Scapa Pier, where there was a connecting bus for Kirkwall market, and also operated to Burray.

The opening of the road along the Churchill Barriers in 1945 meant there was no longer a need for shipping services from Burray and St Margaret's Hope to Mainland, Orkney.

Stevie Mowat, trading as Hoy Ferries, ran the wooden-hulled passenger launch *Jessie Ellen*, which had formerly operated on Loch Ness and Loch Etive, from Stromness to Moaness on Hoy and Graemsay in the summer months from 1976 until the advent of the car ferry *Graemsay* in 1996. A smaller vessel, *Scapa Ranger*, operated the route in the winter months. *Jessie Ellen* was initially chartered by the Orkney Islands Shipping Company from 2 July until 25 September 1976 after *Hoy Head* lost her passenger certificate.

The car ferry came to the South Isles in 1976 with the purchase of the Faeroese ferry *Sam*, built in 1970. She was renamed *Lyrawa Bay* and entered service on 27 September, sailing thrice weekly from Longhope to Lyness, Flotta and Scapa and thrice weekly from Longhope to Flotta, Lyness, Graemsay and Stromness. Vehicles were initially crane-loaded before the linkspans were built in 1983 at all calls apart from Graemsay, where vehicles are crane-loaded to this day. On 3 April 1978, she had a minor engine room fire en route from Longhope to Lyness and had to be towed to her destination by a tug. She was then towed back to Longhope by *Hoy Head* and was out of service until early August for repair. From the building of the terminal at Houton in 1983, she operated from there to Lyness and Flotta; Graemsay only having a weekly call. She was a spare ferry after the purchase of *Geira* in 1986, and was withdrawn in September 1991 and later sold and rebuilt for use as a workboat in connection with a fish farm. She later moved to the Clyde where she continues to be used as a tender and workboat for Offshore Workboats on charter to tug operator Svitzer.

In April 1986, the Shetland Islands Council ferry *Geira* of 1973 was purchased, becoming the third *Hoy Head* in April 1987. She was renamed *Hoy Head II* in 1994, and was sold to owners in Gabon, West Africa to operate from Libreville. However, this fell through and she was sold in 1994 to Reid Marine of Orkney for survey work. She was moved to Ramsgate in that year and renamed *Task One* for harbour duties as a tug assisting a dredger there in 1995. She was joined in August 1991 by the new *Thorsvoe*, built by the Campbeltown Shipyard, which ran from Houton to Lyness on Hoy and Flotta.

The Stromness-based passenger vessel *Guide* (1954) was chartered in 1992 to cover *Golden Mariana*'s overhaul, and was purchased in 1995 for the Graemsay and North Hoy service until *Graemsay* was completed in 1996. In 1995 and 1996, she was on the Westray–Papa Westray shuttle service after mid-September each year on an on-demand basis. She was sold to Roving Eye Enterprises of Houton and fitted with underwater viewing facilities to view the sunken German fleet; since 2011, she has operated out of Macduff on wildlife watching tours and angling trips.

A fourth *Hoy Head* entered service in April 1994. She gives Lyness six sailings a day, Flotta five sailings a day and overnights at Longhope. *Thorsvoe* is now used as a reserve vessel. *Hoy Head* went to the Cammell Laird yard at Birkenhead in early 2013 to be re-engined and lengthened by 13.4 metres.

In 1996, the small car ferry *Graemsay* was built for the route from Stromness to Graemsay and Moaness at the north of Hoy, entering service on 21 June. She has no ramps, the two cars carried being crane-loaded. She was lengthened by 5 metres at Macduff during the 2009/2010 winter.

Orkney Ferries continue to give a lifeline service to the outlying islands of the Orkneys. In the year to 31 March 2014 they carried 328,305 passengers and 85,023 vehicles with their nine ferries. Fortunately, they seem to have been spared the tendering process that has disrupted ferry service elsewhere.

The current fleet is:

Name	Built	Gross Tons	Length	Pass	Cars	Route
Golden Marina	1973	33	16.2m	40	0	Westray-Papa Westray
Eynhallow	1987	104	26.2m	95	8	Tingwall–Rousay–Egilsay–Wyre
Shapinsay	1989	219	36.2m	91	12	Kirkwall–Shapinsay
Varagen	1989	920	50.0m	144	33	Kirkwall–North Isles
Earl Sigurd	1990	771	45.3m	190	26	Kirkwall–North Isles
Earl Thorfinn	1990	771	45.3m	190	26	Kirkwall–North Isles
Thorsvoe	1991	400	35.0m	122	16	spare ferry, summer South Isles
Hoy Head	1994	358	53.0m	125	24	Longhope
Graemsay	1996	82	21.0m	73	2	Graemsay

The steamer *Saga*, which ran from Stromness to Longhope from 1893 until 1895, laid up at Port Bannatyne on Bute in the 1930s.

Robert Garden's *Endeavour*, which ran from Scapa to the South Isles from 1889 to 1928, at Kirkwall after dieselisation in 1913.

Endeavour, to the left, and the first *Hoy Head* off Cava, prior to 1913.

The first *Hoy Head*, which was in service from Stromness to the South Isles from 1896 right up until 1956.

The steam coaster *Wisbech*, operated by Bremner & Co. from 1943 to 1952.

The South Isles steamer *Orcadia*, which was in service from 1947 until 1958.

Bremner & Co.'s coaster *Orkney Dawn*, which ran for them from 1953 to 1955, used to carry scrap from dismantled war installations southbound to mainland UK, and coal northbound.

Deedon (1916), which became Bremner's second *Orkney Dawn* in 1955, only operating for two years.

Finvoy (1924), only made three voyages for Bremner & Co. after her purchase in 1957 before suffering a boiler failure.

The former MFV *Hoy Head*, which operated for Bremner & Co. from 1958 until 1987, seen in 1968.

Zenobia, the former *Hoy Head*, at Millport in 2002.

Watchful, another former MFV, operated for Bremner & Co. from 1961 until 1976.

Jessie Ellen at Inverness, from where she operated from 1961 to 1966.

Countess Cadogan, formerly on the Shannon, which ran from Stromness to Longhope for Captain Robert Arcus from 1921 to 1928, seen here at Stromness.

Countess Cadogan at Killaloe on the River Shannon, 1897.

Cormorant (1885), which operated as a floating shop for Robert Garden from 1898 to 1934, and then for a further four years for John Laird of Burray.

The steamer *Sutors* (1913), which ran for John Laird of Burray from Burray to Kirkwall and St Margaret's Hope from 1925 until 1938.

The Girvan–Ailsa Craig steamer *Ailsa* (1906), which ran for John Laird from Burray from 1938 until the war, at the jetty at Ailsa Craig, *c.* 1911.

Lyrawa Bay (1970), the first car ferry in the South Isles, which operated from 1976 to 1991, at Stromness in 1979.

Guide (1954) lying in Kirkwall Harbour around 1995.

The car ferry *Thorsvoe* at Kirkwall in 1999.

The small car ferry *Graemsay* at Stromness in 1999.

Chapter 8

Shetland Inter-Island Steamers and Ferries

Shetland Island Council car ferry *Fivla* in 1980.

Prior to the introduction of the first *Earl of Zetland* in 1877, the Shetland Steam Shipping Company operated the small screw steamer *Chieftain's Bride* from Lerwick to the North Isles of Shetland from 1868 onwards. She had been built in 1866 by Kirkpatrick & McIntyre of Port Glasgow for John Martin of Iona and had operated from Glasgow to Iona and Tiree. She was hopelessly underpowered, only having an 18 hp engine, and was known locally as 'the Crab', because when caught by strong tides she moved sideways. She was described as 'trash' in a letter from Alexander Sandison, the company's agent in Unst, but in spite of that she became the first steamer to serve the Northern Isles of Shetland. In 1876, the company was renamed Shetland Islands Steam Navigation Company. *Chieftain's Bride* had lost her passenger certificate and *Lady Ambrosine* was chartered from John McCalllum's Western Isles Steam Packet Co. Ltd for five months. The service then reverted to sailing smacks at the beginning of 1877 for three and a half months until *Earl of Zetland* entered service. *Earl of Zetland* was built in 1877 by John Fullerton & Co. at Paisley and had a very long career on the service.

The Overland Route

From the late 1930s up until the advent of the car ferry, there was a motor-boat service across Yell Sound from Mossbank to Ulsta, connecting with a bus service from Lerwick to Mossbank, the whole journey being known as the 'overland route'. After the pier at Toft was opened in 1951, it replaced Mossbank. The boats used were *Donmile*, *Tirrick*, formerly *Norseman* on the Bluemull Sound service (which was sold to run from Burra to Scalloway), *Tystie*, which was built for the service and *Puffin*, the latter used as a spare boat. *Puffin* caught fire and was replaced by *Osprey*, and *Shalder* later replaced *Tystie* on the route, now operated by North Isles Ferries Ltd, until the introduction of car ferries in 1973. *Shalder* was then sold to Orkney to operate from Tingwall to Rousay, Egilsay and Wyre.

The overland route continued across the Bluemull Sound from Belmont to Gutcher on Yell. The vessels used were named *Norseman*, *Viking*, *Osprey* and *Tystie*. *Viking* also operated on the Yell Sound and *Osprey* was the spare boat on the Yell Sound. *Tystie* lasted until the advent of the car ferry *Geira* on the route in 1973 and was then sold to Lerwick Harbour Trust for the Bressay service. Later, she was sold to a private owner on Bressay, where she broke free from her moorings during a gale and was driven ashore, extensively damaged and never repaired.

Bressay

On the route from Lerwick to Bressay there was a motor boat service from 1935 onwards by Black & Williamson with *Norna* and *Brenda*, the latter a converted pinnace from the German First World War battleship, *Hindenburg*. They were taken over by Kirkpatrick and Moncrieff in 1964, who added *Viking Queen*. The service was taken over by the Highlands and Island Development Board in November 1972, then by the Bressay Ferry Service Joint Committee, comprising Zetland County Council, Lerwick Town Council and Bressay District Council in 1973, and, in turn, by Lerwick Harbour Trust in November 1973. The two older boats were replaced initially by the pilot launch *Budding Rose* and later by *Tystie*, transferred from the Bluemull Sound. She remained on the route until the car ferry *Fivla* was introduced on 13 October 1975.

The Car Ferries

In 1973, five ferries of the Norwegian style were ordered by Zetland County Council for new services to replace the *Earl of Zetland*. *Fivla* entered service on the Yell Sound route on 21 May 1973, and *Geira* on the Bluemull Sound service on 20 November 1973. These were built in the Faeroe Islands along with sisters *Fylga* and *Thora*, the final two entering service in January and September 1975 respectively. Two of these ferries were normally used on the Yell Sound service from Toft to Ulsta, although *Fylga* operated from Laxo to Whalsay until 1980. From December 1975, the Gutcher–Belmont service also included some sailings to Oddsta on Fetlar. The *Earl* had called at Brough Lodge on Fetlar, where the remains of the flit-boat still lie on the shore.

Fivla was withdrawn in 1982, sold to the Newfoundland and Labrador Government and renamed *Island Joiner*. She operated in Green Bay from Long Island to Piller's Island until June 2011, when she was replaced on the route by *Sound of Islay*, originally owned by Western Ferries. She was then sold to a private individual in Florida for use as a yacht.

Geira was moved to the Bressay service October 1974 and was sold to the Orkney Islands in April 1986, becoming the third *Hoy Head*.

Thora remains in the fleet as a stand-by vessel, and also sometimes serves Papa Stour in the summer months.

Fylga was sold to MMW Marine Services Ltd in October 2005 and converted for use as a workboat.

The fifth vessel in the quintet was *Grima*, built at Bideford in Devon, which entered service on 28 February 1974 as spare vessel on the Yellsound service, operating as the second ferry there in the summer months. She was chartered to the North Company for the Lerwick–Whalsay service from February 1975 until the car ferry terminals were ready at Laxo and Symbister on 30 January 1976. She later operated on the Lerwick–Bressay service, was the second ferry to Whalsay in 1993, and then a spare ferry until sold in 2004 to Manson Marine of Lerwick for use as a workboat. She was sold on to Venture Marine of Peterhead in 2011.

In 1975, *Thora* and *Fylga* were on the Yellsound service, with *Geira* on the Bluemull Sound, and *Fivla* on the Bressay route. Following the end of *Grima*'s charter to the North Company in January 1976, she went to the Bressay service; *Fivla* went to Yellsound and *Fylga* moved to the Whalsay service. From July 1993 *Fylga* was on a dedicated service from Gutcher to Fetlar.

In February 1975, the converted MFV *Spes Clara*, formerly *Ashgrove*, built in 1947 by Herd & McKenzie at Buckie, entered service for Zetland County Council, operating to Skerries, initially from Symbister on Whalsay. She sailed from Lerwick from 16 March 1976 and offered a twice-weekly service until being replaced by *Filla* in November 1983. She then became a spare vessel and was used for cargo sailings to the islands. She was also used as navigation light tender at Sullom Voe, and served Papa Stour for a time. She was sold in 2003 to a private owner at Scalloway and was broken up in 2012.

On 1 May 1975, local government reorganisation saw Zetland County Council and Lerwick Town Council merge to from Shetland Islands Council.

By the time all the services had commenced in 1976, the vessels were allocated as follows:

Yell Sound: *Fivla* and *Thora*;
Bluemull Sound and Fetlar: *Geira*
Whalsay: *Fylga*
Bressay: *Grima*
Skerries: *Spes Clara*.

In 1980, the 1957-built Norwegian ferry *Kjella* was purchased from Torghattan A/S to replace *Fylga* on the Laxo–Whalsay service. She was rebuilt by enclosing the working alleyway and by converting below-decks cabins to a large saloon prior to her entering service. After the arrival of *Filla* in 1983, she was on the Yell

Sound service and used as a spare ferry. She remained in service as the second ferry on the Whalsay service until her final sailing on 16 June 1998. She was sold later that year to Babcock Material Management of Rosyth for scrapping, but before this could be done she was resold to Quest Underwater Services of Weymouth. In 2000 she was sold to the shipyard Crosscomar at Algeciras in Spain for use as a workboat.

In 1982, a new ferry for the Whalsay service, *Hendra*, was built by McTay Marine in Bromborough. In certain weather conditions Vidlin is used as the mainland terminal rather than Laxo.

In 1983, *Filla* was built at a yard in Flekkefjord, Norway for the service to Skerries. She was a different style of vessel to the other car ferries, had a forwards superstructure and space for only six cars and twenty passengers. She replaced *Spes Clara* and ran from both Lerwick and Vidlin. In August 2003 she was renamed *Snolda*, re-engined, and moved to the route from West Burrafirth to Papa Stour on the west of Shetland.

In 1985, a second *Fivla* was built for the Bluemull Sound service at the Ailsa yard at Troon.

A second *Geira* was built in 1988 by Richard Dunston at Hessle on the Humber. She was used on the Yellsound service.

Another car ferry, *Bigga*, joined the fleet in 1991, replacing *Thora* which became the spare ferry. She was the first ferry in the fleet with three lanes of car space and served on the Yell Sound service until 2004 when she became a spare vessel.

On 14 November 1992 a new double-ended ferry, *Leirna*, built by Ferguson of Port Glasgow to replace *Grima* on the Bressay service, entered service. She can carry nineteen cars and ninety-six passengers and has more extensive passenger accommodation than the other ferries.

A new ferry named *Linga* was built by Stocznia Polnocna at Gdansk in 2002 to replace *Thora* on the Whalsay service.

A new *Filla* for the Skerries route, also built in Gdansk, entered service on 19 June 2003. She is 8 metres longer than her predecessor, and is of a similar design with a conventional bow and stern ramp, and can supply the Skerries with water in times of drought.

2004 saw the introduction of two new larger ferries for the Yell Sound service, *Daggri* and *Dagalien*. Both were built at the Northern Shipyard in Gdansk and have a capacity of 144 passengers and thirty-one cars. They entered service on 17 July and 22 August 2004 respectively. Also in 2004, the terminal at Fetlar was relocated from Oddsta to Hamar's Ness.

Papa Stour

Papa Stour is situated a short distance from west coast of the island of Mainland and has a population of less than twenty. The mailboat *Venture* served Papa Stour from Melby until she sank in a gale on 26 September 1981, with the loss of one life. She was replaced by the fishing boat *Ivy Leaf*, chartered by Shetland Islands Council, which ran from West Burrafirth and served on the route until replaced in 1986 by *Good Shepherd III*, renamed *Koada*, which operated from West Burrafirth to Papa Stour until 2004, when she was sold for use as a charter vessel. *Spes Clara* offered a summer service to Papa Stour from 1993 and was replaced by *Snolda*, formerly the first *Filla*, in 2003.

Foula

Foula lies in an isolated position 27 miles east of Scalloway and has a population of thirty-eight. *Advance*, powered by sail and oars, was on the route from Walls to Foula until replaced by the motor vessel *Island Lass* in 1950, which was lost on 3 March 1962. She was abandoned by her four-man crew in a storm and drifted to off Papa Westray in Orkney when she was taken in tow by the Northern Lighthouse Board ship, *Pole Star* and later sank. A wooden box containing four loaves, newspapers, and £6 3s 5d in change for Betty Humphrey of Foula was washed ashore on the Holm of Papa on Papa Westray. It was noted that Kirkwall Coastguard said the money was being sent to her.

She was replaced by the first of two successive boats called *Westering Homewards*, a converted RNLI lifeboat. The service was taken over by Shetland Islands Council in 1978, although local operators continued to run the vessel. She had a major rebuild, including a new deckhouse and engine, from the end of August 1979 and was replaced by *Spes Clara* during the work. In 1990, the pier at Foula was rebuilt and a new lift supplied to lift the mailboat out of the water at low tide. A new small passenger vessel, *Westering Homewards I*, was built by Jones at Buckie, with the hull constructed in the Netherlands, for the Walls–Foula service in 1990, with a planned speed of 18 knots. In the event, she could only make 13 knots, and she was rejected as being too slow and not reaching her contract speed. She never operated for the council and was eventually sold to the North Atlantic Fishery and Training College at Scalloway for use a workboat, renamed *Moden-Dy*. Sailings to Foula were maintained from West Burrafirth by *Koada* from the withdrawal of *Westering Homewards I* in 1990 until 1996. Some sailings in summer 1995 were operated from Walls. The restricted dimensions of the harbour at Foula have limited the size of vessel which can serve the island. Another small passenger boat, *New Advance*, was built in 1996 at Stromness for the Foula Service and entered service in November of that year.

The Foula service was taken over by Atlantic Ferries in 2006 and is now operated by BK Marine.

Fair Isle

Fair Isle lies 25 miles south of Sumburgh Head and has a population of around seventy. A service to Fair Isle has been operated since 1936 by a series of four vessels named *Good Shepherd*, operated as a community-owned service. *Good Shepherd I* was wrecked in North Haven at Fair Isle on 31 January 1937, her successor operating until 1972, when she was replaced by *Good Shepherd III* (1969); all three were converted fishing vessels. This service was taken over by Shetland Islands Council around 1984 and a new vessel, similar in design and named *Good Shepherd IV*, was built for the route by James Miller & Co. of St Monans, although she was prefabricated by McTay Marine. The service runs weekly from Grutness, with a fortnightly sailing in the summer from Lerwick. On 28 August 1990, she sailed from Scalloway to Foula on charter to British Telecom to take equipment there.

The current fleet comprises:

Name	Built	Gross Tons	Length	Pass	Cars	Route
Thora	1975	147	25.2m	93	10	spare ferry
Hendra	1982	248	33.6m	95	18	Laxo–Symbister, Whalsay
Snolda	1983	170	24.4m	12	6	West Burrafirth–Papa Stour
Fivla	1985	230	30.0m	95	15	spare and stand-by ferry
Good Shepherd IV	1986	76	18.3m	12	1	Lerwick and Grutness to Fair Isle
Geira	1988	230	30.0m	95	15	Bluemull Sound (Belmont, Yell–Gutcher, Unst and Hamars Ness, Fetlar)
Bigga	1991	274	33.5m	96	21	Bluemull Sound (Belmont, Yell–Gutcher, Unst and Hamars Ness, Fetlar)
Leirna	1992	420	34.4m	126	20	Lerwick–Mayfield, Bressay
New Advance	1996	21	9.9m	12	1	Walls–Foula
Linga	2002	658	38.0m	95	16	Laxo–Symbister, Whalsay
Filla	2003	356	35.5m	30	10	Vidlin–Skerries, with a weekly sailing from Lerwick
Dagalien	2004	1,861	64.5m	144	31	Yell Sound (Toft, Mainland to Ulsta, Yell)
Daggri	2004	1,861	65.4m	144	31	Yell Sound (Toft, Mainland to Ulsta, Yell)

Geira, one of the quartet of Faroese-built Shetland ferries, in 1980.

Thora on the Yellsound service in 1986.

The Bideford-built *Grima* in 1980.

The Norwegian-built *Kjella* (1957) departs Lerwick in 1980.

Fivla (1985) on trials on the Clyde.

The Skerries ferry *Filla* at Lerwick in 1992.

The second *Fivla* (1985) at Gutcher, the Yell terminal of the Bluemull Sound service, in 1999.

The second *Geira* in 1999.

Bigga on the Yell Sound service in 1999.

The car deck of *Bigga* in 1999.

Hendra and *Filla* at Vidlin in 1989.

The Bressay ferry *Leirna* fitting out at Ferguson's at Port Glasgow in 1992.

Leirna at Bressay.

The Yell Sound ferry *Daggri* of 2004.

Daggri's sister *Dagalien*, in a storm in 2011, in a photo by Ivan Reid.

The old Bressay passenger ferry *Brenda* at Lerwick in 1985.

The Fair Isle mail boat *Good Shepherd III*, a former fishing boat which served from 1972 until 1986.

Good Shepherd IV, purpose-built for the Fair Isle service in 1986, seen at the tiny harbour at Fair Isle in that year.

The former MFV *Spes Clara* (1947), which served the Skerries from 1976 until 1983 and was later on the Papa Stour service.

Spes Clara at Papa Stour on 17 April 1989.

The abortive Foula vessel *Westering Homewards* of 1991, which never entered service for the island.

The current Foula ferry, *New Advance*, arriving at Walls. (Sidney Sinclair)

New Advance secured safely in her lift at Foula.

Filla 'II' departs Out Skerries.

Acknowledgements

My thanks are due to Iain Quinn and Ian Somerville for the loan of photographs, including some from the collection of the late Alastair McRobb. Thanks are also due to Fraser MacHaffie for the two photos of *Countess of Bantry* and to Norman Tait for the photo of *Ailsa* at Ailsa Craig from the Kirk Collection at Glasgow University. Thanks to Shetland Islands Council's Infrastructure Services Department for the photos of *Linga*, *Daggri* and *Dagalien*. Other photographs are my own and from my own collection.

The Clyde River Steamer Club's annual *Review*, published every year since 1965, has been invaluable for the details of the vessels' operation in that period.

Thanks, as always, are due to my friend Iain Quinn for encouragement and for his diligent proof-reading skills.